STRETCHIN' the BLUES

By Duke Robillard

ISBN 978-1-4234-6771-7

HAL•LEONARD®
CORPORATION
7777 W. BLUEMOUND RD. P.O. BOX 13819 MILWAUKEE, WI 53213

In Australia Contact:
Hal Leonard Australia Pty. Ltd.
4 Lentara Court
Cheltenham, Victoria, 3192 Australia
Email: ausadmin@halleonard.com.au

Visit Hal Leonard Online at
www.halleonard.com

CONTENTS

DOUBLE STOPS
Dress Up the Blues with Piano-Style Licks

Two of my all-time favorite guitarists, Billy Butler and Bill Jennings, made great use of double stops (two notes played at once) to create cool melodies for songs and to spice up their solos. In fact, Billy Butler would sometimes play entire solos constructed of double stops. The following example is from a tune of mine called "Shufflin' with Some Barbeque," from the album *Swing*.

The opening phrase is something I use often, beginning with the root note on the D string (G), then sliding into the 3rd and 5th of the G7 chord from a half step below. That minor 3rd-to-major 3rd movement (Bb to B; spelled as A♯ to B in the example for easier reading) is quite common in the blues, but the accompanying sharp 4th-to-perfect 5th slide (C♯ to D) adds more grease to the griddle. The phrase continues with your ring finger fretting the C and E together, after which comes a slide that uses the middle and ring fingers to move from the 6th to the b7th of the chord (E to F), with the ♯4th-to-5th movement underneath. Grab that high G on the E string to set yourself up for the next slide. To get a good, clear sound, it's important that your right hand plays all downstrokes.

You'll notice that when we come upon the IV (C7) chord, I use this exact same phrase, moving the pattern up to the 10th fret C for measures 5 and 6, but then come down again to G. The song moves along from there with a few variations of these cool, piano-sounding double stops on the V–IV–I chord changes in measures 9–11 and ends on a jazzy D7 chord with all the trimmings. This melody and all its parts can be rearranged to flavor a solo, or be used as a comping tool for any standard blues with a V–IV chord change.

TRACK 1

Moderately (♩♩ = ♩♪)

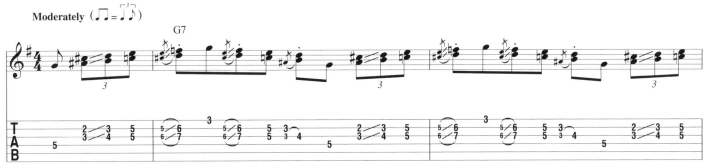

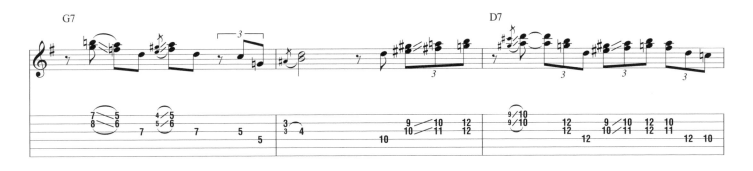

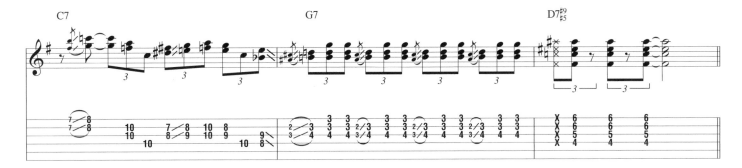

DOUBLE-STOP SOLOING
Mixing It Up to Create Magic

Continuing the theme from Lesson 1, I'd like to show you a guitar solo that consists almost entirely of double stops, with a few single-note lines and passing chords mixed in for variety.

When you play the following solo, you'll notice that I often use half-step motion, sliding my double stops from above or below a position, and usually landing on targeted chord tones. For example, the first phrase begins with a typical single-note line that quickly ascends to a double-stop slide from F♯ and C♯ up to G and D—the root and 5th of G7. The very next double stop of that same measure has a real bluesy sound that comes from sliding in and out of the ♭7th and ♭5th of the chord. I love that sound and use it often in this solo.

Check out the fourth measure, where I incorporate another slide—this time, into the passing chord, D♭7—which then resolves on beat 1 of the next bar. That helps create some nice tension and release going to the IV (C7) chord. In measure 8, I use a passing chord for the same effect, walking down in half steps from a G triad to land on D7 on beat 1 of the following measure. It's a simple move that sounds great and should be in your bag of tricks.

One more thing that I'd like to highlight occurs in measure 9, where I play the E♭7/B♭–D7/A chord change. Instead of the root, I have the 5th of each chord in the bass, which is not an entirely common thing to do, but it adds a more sophisticated, jazzy sound to the V chord.

There are a variety of double-stop riffs in this solo to experiment with, so I hope this lesson gives you some fresh ideas to incorporate into your own playing. Just learn a few of these patterns and mix them with your own single-note lines to create a tasty little solo.

Moderately slow (♫ = ♩♪)

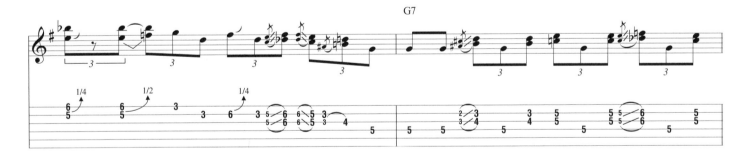

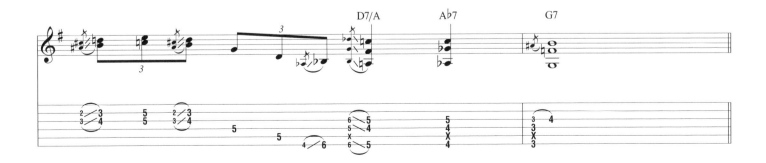

CHROMATIC PASSING TONES
Playing Outside the Box

In this lesson, we're going to explore the use of chromatic passing tones in a swing/ blues solo to demostrate how you can use notes outside the standard pentatonic and dominant scales to create great melodies. Les Paul is a guitarist who regularly incorporated chromatic passages into his playing. Throughout the years, his melodic sense has been an inspiration, which is why I have learned to apply some of his basic ideas into my blues and jazz playing. In fact, they've become an important part of my riff arsenal. Now let's try to make them a part of yours.

The following example is a series of riffs that is played over the first four bars of a B♭ blues and leads up to the IV (E♭9) chord in measure 5. We begin in the first measure with an introductory riff that uses notes from the B♭ major pentatonic scale, including the 3rd (D) and 6th (G). For the purpose of building a melodic blues solo, it's a good idea to think of the ♭7th (A♭) as a passing tone to get from the I chord to the IV chord, rather than highlighting it in your I-chord riff. That's why I went to the G instead.

The second riff is where the chromatic fun begins. I used as many consecutive notes as I could, breaking them up on occasion to make the statement that every note can be used melodically in a series of phrases, even in the blues. The trick to making these chromatic passages work and keep them from wandering is to occasionally hit targeted chord tones on strong beats. That gives the line solid direction and resolves the dissonance of notes outside the scale. A good example is the third measure, where, after descending through a series of passing tones, I land on the 3rd of B♭7 (D) on beat 1, and then continue on down to the root on beat 3.

Play this example in several different keys to help you get the sound in your ears and the notes under your fingers. Then, try to create some of your own melodic passing-tone riffs, which can be as simple as adding one or two chromatic notes in between two scale tones or playing as many as you like. Just remember to keep it tasty!

TRACK 3

THE DIMINISHED PASSING CHORD
Jazzing Up the Blues

In Lesson 3, we talked about using chromatic passing tones and began developing the first four bars of a blues solo. I'd like to continue from where we left off on the IV chord to introduce a diminished passing lick that's sure to add extra spice to your blues recipe.

The example begins with a simple ascending run that clearly outlines the E♭7 (IV) chord from the root on up, including the 3rd, 5th, 6th, and ♭7th (G, B♭, C, and D♭, respectively). Instead of starting on the root, I slide into the E♭ from a half step below to get the swing feel happening and to set up a motif that I use again in the next phrase. The diminished passing chord comes in measure 2—bar 6 of the 12-bar blues form—where I again slide up a half step to the root (E), and then climb in consecutive minor 3rds all the way up to G on fret 8 of the B string.

Besides being a tasty-sounding lick, that diminished run is a great way to resolve back to the I chord from the IV, because E°7 acts as a passing chord that leads to B♭7. In fact, if you look at some of the notes in that diminished chord—for example, E, G, and D♭—you'll notice that each is exactly a half step below a chord tone in B♭7. The E wants to resolve up to F, the 5th of B♭7; the G wants to resolve up to A♭, the ♭7th; and the D♭ wants to resolve up to D♮, the 3rd. All three notes are pulling to that ol' I chord. Notice that I resolve to the I chord by descending chromatically to the 5th (F).

In the third and fourth measures, I play a lick that has sort of a back-and-forth motion as it heads down the major scale and to the Cm7 (ii) chord. That kind of motion makes the phrase swing in a way that reminds me of something Tiny Grimes might have played back in the 1940s. It's fairly straightforward, but a simple guitar statement like that can sometimes be the sweetest-sounding phrase in your entire solo.

AMAZING GRACE NOTES
A Device to Emulate Sax and Trumpet Players

In Lesson 4, we reached the final four bars of our 12-bar form, comprised of a ii–V (Cm7–F7) progression and then a I–vi–ii–V (B♭6–Gm7–Cm7–F7) turnaround to wrap up the chorus. This section provides an opportunity to go out in style with some hip lines.

After stating the ii (Cm7) chord by way of a half-step accent chord (D♭m7), I run up a Cm7 arpeggio from the root. Notice that the low C note is preceded by a B♮, which provides a nice bit of color. The final B♭ of the Cm7 arpeggio resolves by half step to A, the 3rd of F7 (the V chord). I've added a bluesy touch here via a half-step grace-note slide into the A note. After continuing up an F7 arpeggio (F–A–C–E♭), I throw in a signature riff that is rooted in the F *altered scale* (F–G♭–A♭–A–B–C♯–E♭). Since it contains every altered note, it's quite an attention-grabber! The rhythm, articulation, and note choice here is pure bebop.

The final E♭ of measure 2 is resolved by half step to the 3rd (D) of B♭6 (I chord) in measure 3 to begin the I–vi–ii–V turnaround. This is the same device—a ♭7th resolving to a 3rd—I used when moving from Cm7 to F7 earlier. Notice that I target the 6th (G) of B♭6 here; this is a nice alternative at times to the tougher sound of the ♭7th. By learning riffs like these, you're opening up your fingers to a four-fret spread, which helps break out of the minor pentatonic comfort zone. The final riff occurs over the ii–V (Cm7–F7) change of the turnaround and begins (again) by approaching a chord tone (G) of Cm7 from a half step below (F♯). After an ornamental arpeggio figure over Cm7, the ♭7th (B♭) is once again resolved by half step to the 3rd (A) of F7, which is dressed up with yet another grace-note slide.

All these slurred notes help to emulate the sound of some of my favorite sax and trumpet players. It's a technique that I use quite often, along with sometimes raking the pick en route to a target note, to create a sense of swing by slightly lagging in time.

TRACK 5

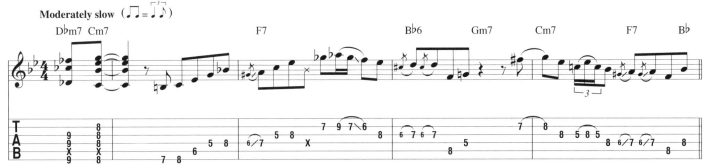

EXPANDING YOUR BLUES OPTIONS
Adding an Extra ii–V Change

There are so many interesting twists that you can add to the blues that it can be a bit daunting at times. However, once you get started by learning one or two variations, you'll begin to realize how closely they're related—and this makes things much easier. One of my favorite variations involves substituting a ii–V chord change in bar 2. In a normal 12-bar blues, you either hang on the I chord through bars 1–4 (called a "slow change") or move to the IV chord in bar 2 and back to the I chord for bars 3–4 (called a "quick change"). In the following example, we're using the quick-change formula, but replacing the IV chord with a ii–V change, which serves the same purpose as the IV chord—i.e., providing a little harmonic motion to break up the extended I chord—but sounds a bit more sophisticated and jazzy.

We begin in bar 1 with a line based on a B♭ arpeggio. Notice how the tonic (B♭) note is *encircled* by the major 7th (A) and 9th (C)—a typical device found in bebop. We lead into bar 2 by way of a chromatic leading tone (F♯), which resolves to G and the ensuing Cm7 arpeggio figure for beats 1 and 2. Another typical bop-sounding phrase is used over the F7 chord, outlining an F7♭9 sound.

We begin bar 3 with some B♭ major pentatonic ideas before stepping down chromatically to the ♭7th (A♭) of the B♭7 chord. In bar 4, we change gears and play some chord punches (B♭13–B♭7♯5) that resolve to the IV (E♭9) chord. As I've demonstrated in previous lessons, inserting these chordal hits at key moments such as this is a nice way to add depth to your playing. Notice the half-step resolutions that occur throughout this example: F♯ to G (end of bar 1), B♭ to A (middle of bar 2), E♭ to D (end of bar 2), and the G–G♭–F line during the chord punches (see the B string). Half-step resolution is the cornerstone of countless jazz lines.

TRACK 6

A MUST-KNOW BLUES INTRO
Taking It From the Five

In the blues world, there are a few standard ways that we can begin a song when up on the bandstand. By far, the most common is to simply start "on the one" (i.e., beat 1 of measure 1). There are many other common intros, though, and it's important to familiarize yourself with as many as possible so you'll be ready when the time comes. In this lesson, I'd like to show you a blues intro known as "taking it from the five."

Just like it sounds, this intro begins on the V chord, which occurs in measure 9 of the 12-bar blues form. That means it's a four-bar phrase, and it's our job in those four bars to create a sense of excitement and to set the mood for the rest of the song. What I'm playing is fairly simple, and it doesn't need to be anything more. The essence of good blues music is tension and release, and this is accomplished with strong note choice, some well-placed bends, and solid resolution at the right time.

The following example opens with a common pick-up phrase that leads from the 5th (G) up to the root note of the key, C. It's kind of like announcing, "This is a slow blues song, baby, and we're in the key of C." I begin the four-bar phrase over the V (G7) chord, with a bit of tension right away, bending the E♭ note up to F. The phrase continues on beat 2 with a run down the C minor pentatonic scale, and for added bite, I bend the first E♭ note up a half step, to E♮ (the 6th of G). Beats 3 and 4 contain speedy triplet runs from the C blues scale, which work their way down to the target note in beat 4 (G).

I lead into the IV (F9) chord in measure 2 with a few chord punches, approaching the F9 chromatically on the downbeat by way of a G♭9. Breaking up your single-note lines with chord punctuations like this makes for a nice change of texture and is especially effective in a trio format. Measure 2 includes a few noteworthy elements. The 4-against-3 rhythm on beats 2 and 3 is a great way to create tension in 12/8 time, as it makes the listener want to hear a return to a triplet-based line. Also note the bluesy quarter-step bends on the E♭ and the inclusion of the A note to start the phrase on beat 2. While most of the lines in this intro are drawn from the C blues scale, that A note works particularly well here because it's part of the F chord.

The tension created from the 4-against-3 rhythms in measure 2 is released convincingly in measure 3 via a classic double-stop phrase from the C blues box position. Notice that the F/A double stop is carefully placed to align with the F7 chord on beat 3. I bring things to a solid conclusion in measure 4 by walking up chromatically on beat 2 to the V (G7/D) chord before finishing off with a D♭9/F-to-C9/E half-step resolution, leaving us at the top of the form.

Taken altogether, I've packed a good amount of concepts into four bars: bends, triplet runs, chromatic lines, double stops, and chord punctuations. It's that kind of variety that helps keep your playing interesting.

TRACK 7

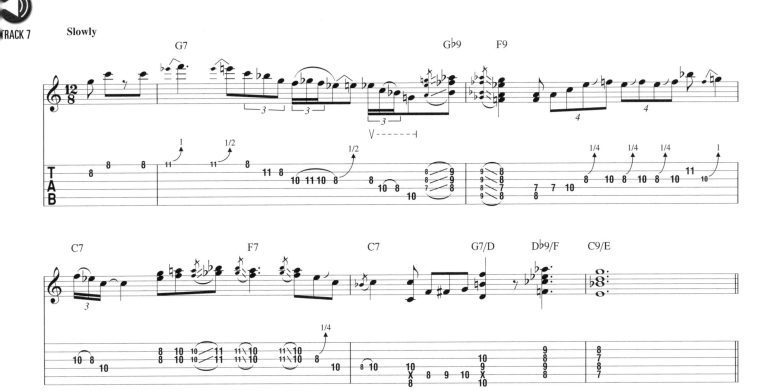

THIS ONE'S FOR LES!
Harmonized Riffs from the Master

Les Paul will be forever remembered as a true pioneer whose contributions to the development of the electric guitar, recording, and music in general were so profound that some say he single-handedly changed the shape of modern music. Besides his numerous ground-breaking inventions, Les left us with a whole library of classic licks, and what better way to pay tribute to the man then by sharing one of those timeless jewels with you here.

The example here can be used as either an intro or an outro for a swing tune in the key of C and is based on a riff that Les played on many recordings through the years. Its sound is somewhat reminiscent of Charlie Christian's pre-bebop guitar style from which Les borrowed many ideas and phrases. He made it completely his own, however, by harmonizing riffs like this one in a unique way, utilizing multiple guitars and his invention: the multi-track recorder. The main guitar part (Gtr. 1) begins with a chromatic climb from C up to E♭, and then descends into a pattern of three diminished arpeggios. Each of these three arpeggios consists of the same four interchanging notes (C–E♭–G♭–A), which clearly outline C°7. Starting on E♭, the second guitar plays the same riff exactly a minor 3rd above Gtr. 1's part to serve as the harmony. This strengthens the diminished sound even further by adding a minor 3rd interval above every note that Gtr. 1 plays.

The second half of this riff begins on the G chord, with Gtr. 1 playing a slick and quick little move—a hammer-on to the A note, followed by a pull-off to G, and then a slide down to F♯ with the first finger. From there, all you have to do to bring it back home is walk up chromatically from G to C, the root of the progression. The harmony part for the second half mimics the main guitar, once again, but this time it's played a major 3rd above Gtr. 1 to fit the implied G chord. Notice that together, the two parts climb from G and B up to C and E, the root and 3rd of the G and C chords, respectively. We finish off with a C6/9 chord in the main part and a C6 shape above, bending them both down a half step with the vibrato bar for cool effect.

Les experimented extensively with diminished, augmented, and whole-tone harmonies, often overdubbing several more than two guitars. In that spirit, try building more harmonies on this example or on your own riffs to find your inner Les Paul.

THE CHARLESTON GROOVE
A Blues Variation

The blues is a form of music with nearly infinite possibilities and variations. As I've shown in previous lessons, there are all sorts of choices in chords, rhythms, and tempos to choose from to create a limitless array of sounds and moods. For this lesson, I'd like to show you a cool rhythmic comping feel for yet another blues variation. I borrowed this groove from an Eddie "Cleanhead" Vinson record with Cannonball Adderley's group. We'll take it in the key of G, which is one of my favorite keys for playing guitar in this style.

At the heart of this rhythm guitar part are the accents on beat 1 and the "and" of beat 2. This type of rhythmic figure is sometimes called the "Charleston groove," and you're bound to come across it many times during your blues and jazz explorations (organists, in particular, play this type of rhythm all the time). For bars 1–3, we answer the G13 chord on beat 1 with one a half step higher, A♭13, on the "and" of beat 2. In bar 4, however, we play a G13–G7♯5 progression, which helps lead to the IV chord. Notice that I use my thumb to play the bass notes that surround all of these chord hits.

When you get to bars 5 and 6, just move the half-step chordal pattern up to the eighth fret for the C13–D♭13 changes. Transposition of I-chord material to the IV chord is an extremely common technique, especially when playing a groove-oriented blues figure. Things get interesting in bar 8, where we descend to the ii (Am7) chord by way of a chromatic bass line: C–B–B♭–A. Notice, however, that we're not just playing the same chord voicings. The first two chords are actually F7/C and E7/B, and the third is B♭m7. The important thing to realize is that E7 is the V of Am7, and *that's* the essence of this chromatic descent: E7 to Am7. Both the F7/C and B♭m7 can be thought of as ornamental chords a half step above.

We round out this blues song with half-step slides into the V (D7) chord and a return to the I–♭II chord riff in bars 11–12. This progression is a great one to solo over, so try jamming on it with a friend.

ACK 9

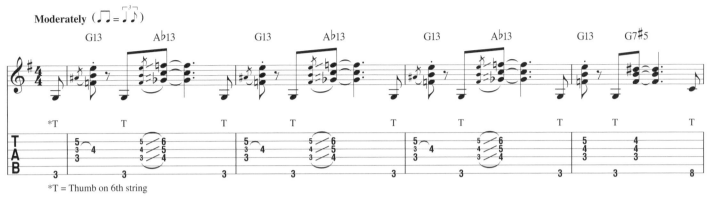

*T = Thumb on 6th string

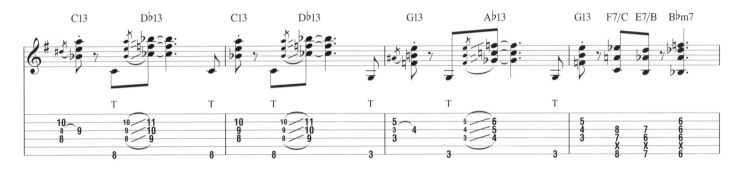

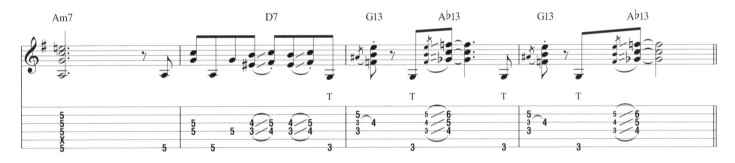

STEAL THIS RIFF!
Building Your Library of Sound

As we travel down the road of music and guitar exploration, we should always be on the lookout for new riffs to steal or borrow from to expand our vocabulary. The point is to build a library of phrases and ideas that we can reference to better express ourselves on guitar. That's not to say that we want to merely string together memorized licks and runs in a solo, but by having a good supply of riffs at our fingertips, we have a stronger starting point for developing melodic ideas of our own. Also, by cultivating a large repertoire of licks, it becomes much easier to hear where certain notes are located before playing them, getting you closer to every guitarist's goal—the ability to play what you hear in your head.

Here's a new phrase for your collection that has a jazzy, bebop flavor and can be used in many situations:

TRACK 10

The phrase basically outlines a I–VI–ii–V progression in the key of Bb (Bb6–G7–Cm7–F7), but I substituted a passing diminished chord (B°7) for the G7 for fun. In fact, this riff outlines the changes so well that there aren't any passing tones, except for the Gb (the b9th) on the F7 chord, which quickly resolves to the root (F). The rest of the example goes like this: root–3rd–5th of Bb6, root–3rd–5th–7th of B°7, 5th–3rd–root–7th of Cm7, and 3rd–b9th–root–7th of F7, ending on D (the 3rd of Bb6). It's important to know that this lick will work great whether the person comping is playing a VI chord or its passing-diminished substitution. Over a G7, the notes in the second half of measure 1 (B–D–F–Ab) become the 3rd, 5th, 7th, and b9th of the chord.

This riff can fit perfectly in any jazz standard with the same type of chord changes; for example, the first couple of bars of "rhythm changes" or a turnaround. It can also work as an intro or outro to a blues when repeated, but I like to use it in the first two bars of a blues as an interesting way to get back to the I chord, leading to the IV (E♭7) chord, as shown below.

Keep in mind that this approach only works well in a jazz-style blues song, where it's appropriate to add extra chords of this nature.

After memorizing this one, go to your music collection and find some more licks to transcribe from your favorite guitarists. The style of music or the type of song doesn't matter because anything you pick up will only add depth to your expanding palette of melodic ideas.

BRINGIN' THE FUNK
Mixing Lead Breaks with Rhythmic Accents

In this lesson, we're going to look at a funky style of blues guitar in which we combine rhythm playing with some lead lines. The approach works especially well in a trio setting, where there's no other harmony instrument to back you up. Below is the head to a tune of mine called "Stratisfied," which is in the key of A and is a perfect example of this kind of playing.

Notice how the switch from lead notes to rhythm is almost seamless throughout. One is an extension of the other in this style, and it allows for a very full sound in a bass, drums, and guitar trio. The melody on the I (A7) chord is derived from mixing the A major pentatonic scale with the A blues scale—a common device in blues. After the lead play in measures 1 and 2, the groove is firmly established with a funky A7 chord riff that uses your thumb on the fifth fret of the low E string. You'll want to barre strings 3 and 4 with your first finger at the fifth fret and be sure to touch the fifth string with either the thumb or first finger (or both) so it doesn't ring out when you strum. (It wouldn't be a bad idea to mute the top two strings, as well.) When you play this style of funky guitar, it's best to let your pick-hand wrist go almost limp and use a loose down-and-up picking motion, creating the accents with stronger pick attacks. Since you have the unused strings muted with the fretting hand, you can strum freely through all six strings if you choose.

Notice that the major 3rd of the key (C♯) is avoided completely over the IV (D7) chord in measures 5–6, as it would clash with the chord's ♭7th, C. The sliding tritone move at the beginning of measure 6 is a slick and economical way to sound seventh-chord harmony, as the destination notes (C and F♯) function as the ♭7th and major 3rd of the IV chord, respectively. The 3rd and 7th are the defining notes of any seventh chord and determine whether it's major, minor, or dominant.

Instead of playing a V-to-IV progression in measures 9 and 10, we're playing a II–V progression: B7–E7. The B7 harmony is implied with a sliding 6ths lick on strings 1 and 3, whereas the E7 chord is basically run over by a descending lick from the A (tonic) blues scale. The 12-bar form is rounded out with a return to the A7 funk groove for measures 11 and 12, filling the space where a turnaround would normally occur.

Remember to keep that wrist nice and loose to get the right feel on your rhythm parts. This type of playing is as much about the sound as it is about the notes.

TRACK 11

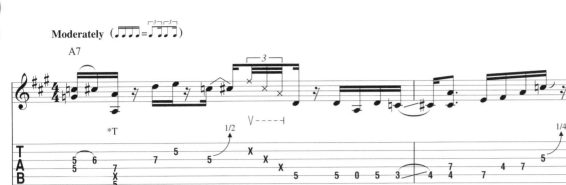

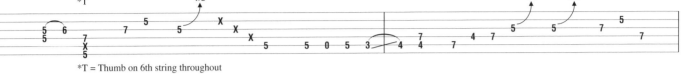

*T = Thumb on 6th string throughout

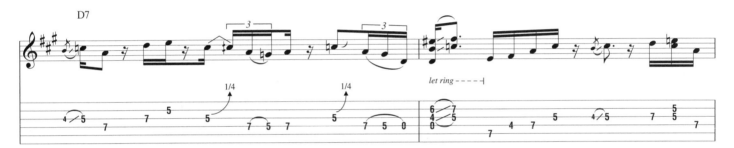

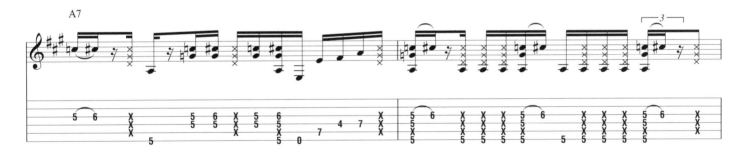

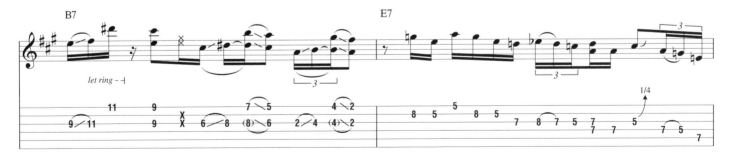

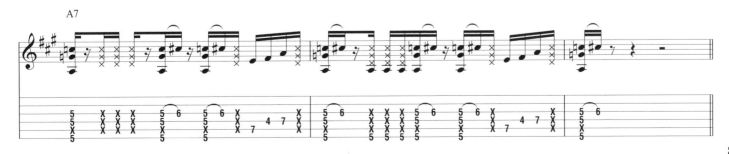

MAKING IT SWING, CHARLIE CHRISTIAN-STYLE
A "Sliding Sixth Chord" Trick for Your Blues Rhythm Bag

Charlie Christian has long been heralded for bringing the guitar out of the rhythm section and into the limelight. His virtuosic, horn-like solos redefined what a guitar could do and influenced countless players since. What's perhaps not as well-known is that he was also an innovative songwriter who wrote or co-wrote many of Benny Goodman's hits during their time together. This lesson is an example of a blues head in his style, using a signature sliding-sixth-chord theme that's become a staple in the blues guitar vocabulary.

What's interesting to note about this tune is that it's very similar to a standard 12-bar blues form, but the IV chord has been doubled in length, as has the I chord that follows, to create a 16-measure form. The meat and potatoes of this blues head is based on what I call a "sliding sixth chord"—a three-note shape that, when moved in whole steps, creates an attractive dominant hook. Notice that the first three-note chord that we slide into in measure 1 (after the three-note pickup lick) contains the notes A♭, C, and F—otherwise known as A♭6. However, when we move this same shape down a whole step, we get G♭, B♭, and E♭. This shape, which could logically be called a G♭6 chord, creates an A♭9 sound when heard over an A♭ bass note. Taken altogether, the effect is basically an A♭ dominant sound, hence the simplified A♭7 chord symbol.

This move is repeated for the IV (D♭7) chord, with the same chords transposed up a 4th. Due to the tuning of the guitar, this, of course, results in different shapes. (If you wanted the shapes to remain the same, you could alternatively move up the neck and play these chords on the same string set (2–4), based off the sixth-string D♭ root at fret 9.) For the turnaround section in measures 13–14, a hip ♭VI–V move adds an unexpected twist. (For ease of reading, the ♭VI chord is spelled enharmonically here as E7, instead of F♭7.) Notice that the voicings we're using at this spot are derived from the top three strings of the typical fifth-string root barre chord form. We bring things to close by resolving to the tonic A♭7 chord with a straight-ahead, eighth-note melodic figure: root–5th–7th–root (A♭–E♭–G–A♭).

The sliding-sixth-chord technique is a great way to jazz up your rhythm playing and it can provide some well-deserved relief from the same old boogie patterns that we're used to. Sometimes all you need is a simple trick like this to add freshness to your music.

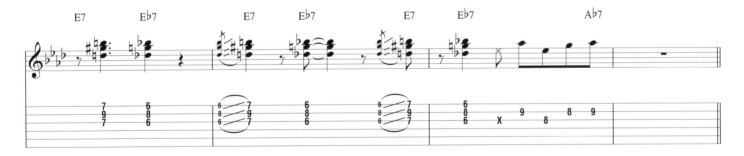

12/8 SLOW BLUES INTRO
Miles of Style in Just Four Bars

Sometimes a great song requires the proper setup—something to set the tone of what's to come and invite the listener along for a ride. This can be especially true for a slow tune, which is why I want to show you a cool slow blues intro in 12/8 time that's sure to set up a song with style.

For those who haven't dealt with a 12/8 feel yet, let's first see if we can shed some light on the matter with a brief explanation: 12/8 is a meter that is common in—but not exclusive to—slow blues songs and in which each measure contains 12 eighth-note beats. The eighth notes are grouped into four sets of three, with an accent on beats 1, 4, 7, and 10.

Because of those accents, you end up with a rhythm that sounds a lot like 4/4 time with a triplet feel, but the continuous triplets stand out more on their own. A couple of great song examples in 12/8 are Jimi Hendrix's "Red House" and Little Walter's "Last Night," but there are many more out there to be found.

Now check out our four-bar blues intro in B♭, as shown below. I use plenty of my signature-style double stops to create a rolling, piano-like sound over the I and IV chords. Almost all of these double stops slide a half step up or down to their targeted chord tones, which contributes to a nice, loose feel. It's important to keep your fretting hand fairly relaxed to achieve that looseness, as well. The turnaround chord progression in the fourth measure is ♭VI–V–♭II–I (G♭7–F7–C♭7–B♭13), which basically means I'm approaching both the V chord and the I chord from a half step above. What makes it sound extra special is the bassline that's created by playing the 5ths in the bass of the first two chords (G♭7/D♭ and F7/C), instead of their root notes. That gives you a steady chromatic descent from D♭ down to B♭.

Normally, I would play an intro like this unaccompanied until the ♭VI–V chord change, leading into the verse, but it would also sound fine for the band to come in right from the top. Try transposing this to other keys so you can play it anywhere on the neck and increase your mastery of the fretboard.

TRACK 13

HEADS UP!
Learn How to Craft a Memorable Blues Head

In this lesson, you're going to learn a swing blues head of mine and we'll use it as an example of how to write your own. For those who don't know, the term "head" is music lingo for main melody or theme. Like many blues heads, this one contains a single phrase that's repeated three times, with slight variations each time to suit the changing harmonies. We're working over a basic jazz-blues progression in the key of C, which, along with the standard I (C7), IV (F7), and V (G7) chords, contains a VI (A7) and a ii (Dm7).

We begin with a descending line based out of the C Mixolydian mode around eighth position. The figure on beats 1 and 2 containing the quick pull-off (B♭–A–G) following the first A note is sometimes called a "turn" and is a staple of the jazz language. The harmony-defining double stops in measures 2 and 3 slide up chromatically to the 3rd and 5th of C7 (E and G, respectively) from a half step below, Charlie Christian-style. (This move was later adopted by B.B. King, Chuck Berry, and countless others.) In measure 4, we cap off the first four-measure phrase and lead to the IV chord with a C13, followed by a C7♭13 for extra tension.

The same riff is then basically repeated in measures 5–8 (as if still over a C), but we lower the 3rd (E) to E♭ so it fits the F7 change. The repetition here makes this melody instantly memorable to the listener by simply reinforcing what they just heard. This phrase ends differently, as we step down to the VI (A7) chord by way of a quick, chromatic B♭7. The A7 functions as the secondary dominant of the ii chord, Dm7, which begins our final phrase (measure 9). The final riff is basically the same as the one in measures 1–3, only we've thinned out the double stop to single notes, and we wrap it up in measure 11 with another jazzy flourish: a B♭–C–B♭–G lick, followed by the leading tone (B♮) and tonic (C).

This kind of repetitive swing riff is a prime example of what "riff jazz," or Kansas City jazz, is all about. Riffs like this can even be used behind a soloist to heighten the intensity. (This particular riff is probably best used as a head or theme, as the number of notes makes it a bit too busy for someone to solo over, but by thinning it out, you could have a great backing riff.) Most big bands employed this concept from time to time, but the Kansas City bands of Jay McShann and Count Basie, as well as Lionel Hampton's big band, became widely known for this type of thing. The concept also greatly influenced the original R&B sound in the '60s.

TRACK 14   **Moderately** (♫ = ♩ ♪)

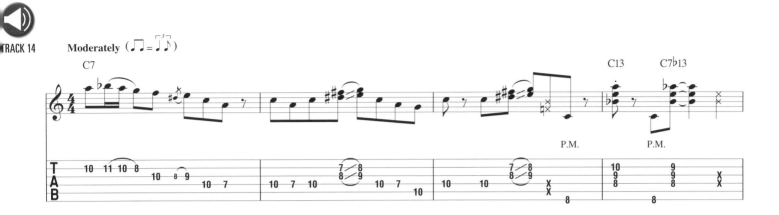

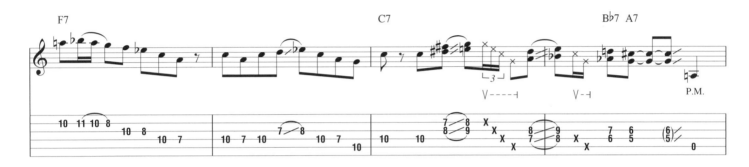

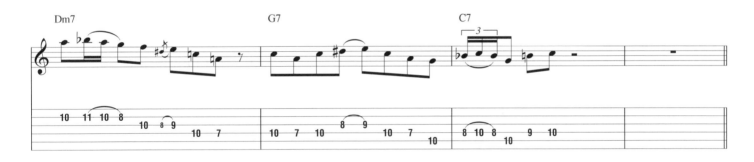

TOOLS OF THE PHRASE

Using Space, Rhythmic Variation,
and Imitation to Create Lead Lines

In case I haven't mentioned it before, playing a great solo is all about mastering the art of phrasing; it's about mixing together the right concoction of timing and melody to create something lyrical, expressive, and hopefully, memorable to the listener. With that in mind, let's take a look at the first four measures of a slow blues in B♭, concentrating on a few different phrasing tools: using space, varying rhythms, and imitation.

We open with a Lester Young–inspired phrase that nicely outlines the B♭ dominant harmony by nicking the A♭ (♭7th) during the descent. Measure 2 begins by imitating beat 1 of measure 1, using the same half-step grace-note slide into a repeated note. The difference is that this time we're sliding into the 5th (F) of B♭7, instead of the root, as in measure 1. This device (imitation) can really lend cohesion to your solos and makes them more memorable to the listener. (People generally enjoy it when they recognize a melody.) Measure 2 finishes off with a classic jazz-blues line from the B♭ major scale (notice that the *major* 7th, A, is used, even though the chord is B♭7). This line is "dressed to the nines," however, with grace-note slides from both directions, lending it a very vocal, fluid sound.

We lay out for pretty much all of measure 3, just sustaining the tonic (B♭) note. The emphasis here is on using space and letting the music breathe. It's a nice way to contrast a quicker line that follows. At the end of measure 3, we illustrate this point with a *double-time lick* (16th notes played over a swinging eighth-note groove) that begins with a chromatic B♭–B♮ line, targeting the C on the downbeat of measure 4. What I'm doing in measure 4 is superimposing a ii–V (Fm7–B♭7) progression based on the IV chord, E♭. Even though the chord is still B♭7, I'm thinking Fm7 (ii of E♭) for the first two beats and B♭7 (V of E♭) for the last two. This is common in jazzier blues styles. Notice that the first three notes on beat 1 outline an Fm triad (C–A♭–F), and the first three notes on beat 3 outline a B♭ triad (F–D–B♭). On the "and" of beat 2, the three-note chromatic legato run up to the 5th (F) is very saxophone-like and is keeping with the Lester Young vibe. Measure 4 ends with another staple of jazz blues: a chromatic descent from the tonic (B♭–A–A♭) that resolves to the 3rd (G) of the IV chord, E♭. Most jazz players have a huge repertoire of ii–V licks. If you know some, you can try plugging them into measure 4 of a blues to shake things up a bit. Remember, though, that it's a ii–V of IV—not a ii–V of the tonic (I) chord.

Slowly

*Played as even sixteenth notes.

BLUES TRANSLATION
New Ideas from Alternate Sources

When looking for inspiration for new licks and riffs, it's only natural that guitarists search out their current favorite guitar hero or book for some ideas. After all, the fundamental way to learn guitar vocabulary is by copying other players of the same instrument. The only problem is that by going to the obvious source every time, we only get one perspective on good lead and rhythm playing. When I practice, I like to think about what kinds of phrases other instruments would play and try to emulate them. In previous lessons, I've illustrated some riffs that were piano-like in their approach, but what about the other instruments on the bandstand? How would an organ comp behind a guitar solo? How would a horn section punctuate a melody line?

With all that in mind, I've come up with a blues head in the key of G, inspired by a call-and-response pattern that might happen between an organ player and a horn section. It features an ascending line through the Mixolydian scale, starting on the 5th of each chord (D on G7), with a double-stop slide at the top. That's followed by a riff that bounces between the root note on the sixth string and a sliding triple-stop shape, which outlines the seventh chord. I approach the triple-stop move two different ways throughout this example, sometimes sliding from a half step below, and other times hammering on. A similar effect is created either way. When the IV and V chords (C7 and D7, respectively) come around, this two-measure riff pattern can simply be moved up the neck to match the changing harmony. The moveable nature of this riff also makes transposition to other keys a breeze.

Guitarists of all styles and levels can find inspiration in the musical ideas played by other instrumentalists. Initially, it can take a little work to translate those sounds to the guitar, but that work will pay off in a big way with an expanded, unique palette of sound.

TRACK 16   Moderately

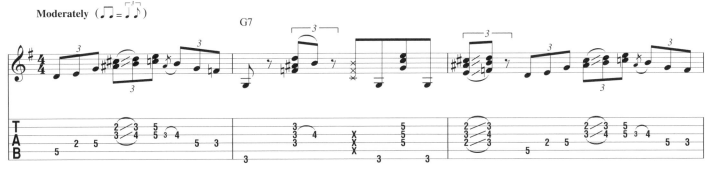

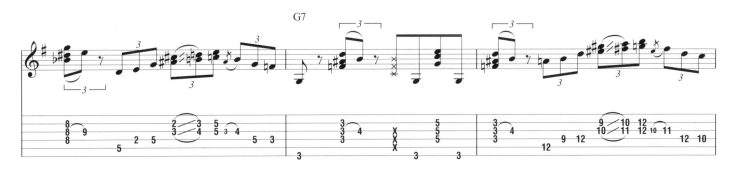

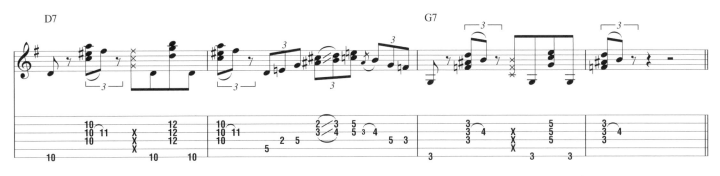

SETTIN' THE TONE
A Multi-functional I–VI–II–V progression in B♭

Let's take a look at a I–VI–II–V progression in B♭ that's extremely versatile. Though I'm thinking of this as an intro, it would work equally well as a turnaround or an outro. You can use this sequence to kick off a number of mid-tempo jazz standards—or even a blues, if your bandmates are up to it. Let's take a quick look at the four chords that are used, in case you're not familiar with them.

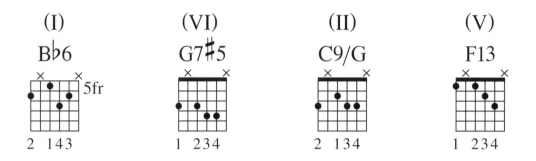

Play through these voicings a few times to get a feel for them before attempting the example. Notice the *voice leading* used in the last three chords: each chord shares a common tone with the chord that follows, and no voice moves more than a whole step. After the G7♯5 chord, we barely move outside of a three-fret span. This lends a smooth quality to the progression—not to mention that it's easy on the fret hand!

Another concept to check out here is *inversion*. Notice the "C9/G" chord symbol. This tells us to play a C9 chord with a G in the bass. A chord is said to be "inverted" when a note other than the root appears in the bass. In this case, the chord is actually a rootless because there is no C. Technically, you could also call this chord a Gm6, and you'd be correct. However, it obviously functions here as a II chord in the key of B♭, so we're thinking of it as "C9 with G in the bass." All of this theory is to point out that, by using this inversion, we're able to maintain the smooth voice leading in the bass, as well.

Now let's get to the riff. I'm playing fingerstyle here and using a repetitive pattern throughout, separating the bass notes from the chord. This simulates a larger ensemble and is a nice way to generate more interest. To increase the separation effect, I'm palm-muting the bass notes on string 6 and allowing the chords on top to ring freely.

Each bass note is approached from a half step below, even if the approach note falls outside the key. This dissonance is accepted by the ear because it goes by quickly and has become a staple of blues and jazz styles. In fact, our ears are quite accustomed to hearing notes slid into from a half step below. To play this riff most efficiently, check out the fingering suggestions in the notation. With the exception of the open low-E string, I'm using my first finger for all of these approach notes and following it with either my second finger (for Bb6 and C9/G) or my first finger again (for G7#5).

This riff is a great little setup that suits a guitar trio or a quartet with piano, guitar, bass, and drums. Try it as an intro to your favorite slow-to-medium swing tune. The bass typically provides a fill at the break that is heard at the end of this example and leads the band into the beginning of the tune.

TRACK 17

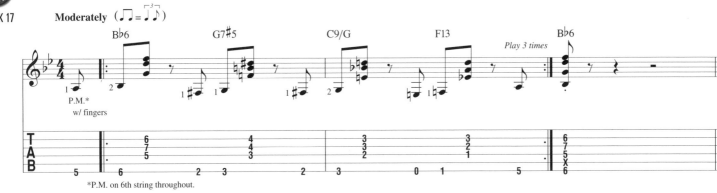

*P.M. on 6th string throughout.

CLOSE-VOICED SWING RIFF, LES-STYLE
Emulate a Brass Section with This Swing Staple

What we have here is a swinging riff reminiscent of Les Paul. This riff is especially nice to use if you're playing in a trio with only a bass and drummer because it creates a full, sophisticated sound. We're using close-voiced harmony on the top three strings to reproduce a Count Basie–like trumpet section in the key of D. If you pull this one off at your local open-mic blues jam, you'll turn some heads for sure. It's also nice for generating momentum that can be carried into the next chorus of your solo.

We start in measure 1 over the I chord, playing the root (D) on string 1, the 6th (B) on string 2, and the 5th (A) on string 3, resulting in a D6 cluster that's a bit of a stretch. Normally, it would be easily playable with a 4–2–1 fingering, low to high, but if you look ahead, you'll see that we need our pinky to reach up for the high F♯ note on string 1. This means we'll need to fret the A–B–D cluster with fingers 3, 2, and 1. After nicking the high F♯, we move the D6 cluster down a half step for beat 2 and back up for beat 3. Be sure to note the staccato articulation on beats 2 and 3, which helps the riff swing. In measure 2, we repeat this move, but the rhythm is condensed to four straight eighth notes, which creates some nice syncopation and makes for some quick finger work. This same idea is repeated for measures 3 and 4. The whole move is quite tricky and will take some practice.

For the IV (G7) chord change in measure 5, we maintain the D on string 1 and B on string 2, but we replace the A on string 3 with an F, which is the ♭7th of G7. This results in a voicing of F–B–D, low to high, or ♭7th–3rd–5th relative to the G7 chord. Keeping with the same motif, we reach up and nick the high F this time, as is fitting over the G7 chord, and follow by moving the F–B–D voicing down a half step and back up again. Again, this move is rhythmically condensed in measure 6 for the syncopated version.

For the V (A7) chord in measures 9–10, we create yet another variation of this motif, again maintaining the D and B on strings 1 and 2, respectively, but substituting G on string 3. This looks like a simple G triad, but when played over an A in the bass, it results in an A9sus4 sound, which gives it a nice, jazzy sound. Maintaining the tonic (in this case, D) over the V chord like this is typical of the "shout choruses" that this riff emulates. We treat this new voicing to the same embellishment as before, hitting the high F on string 1 and continuing on with the half-step moves as before, closing out in measures 11–12 with a recap of the I-chord version found in the opening measures.

These close-voiced riffs are a trademark of swing riffing and work as well on guitar and piano as they do in brass sections. They're a nice way to give the audience something to grab ahold of, which is always a good thing!

TRACK 18

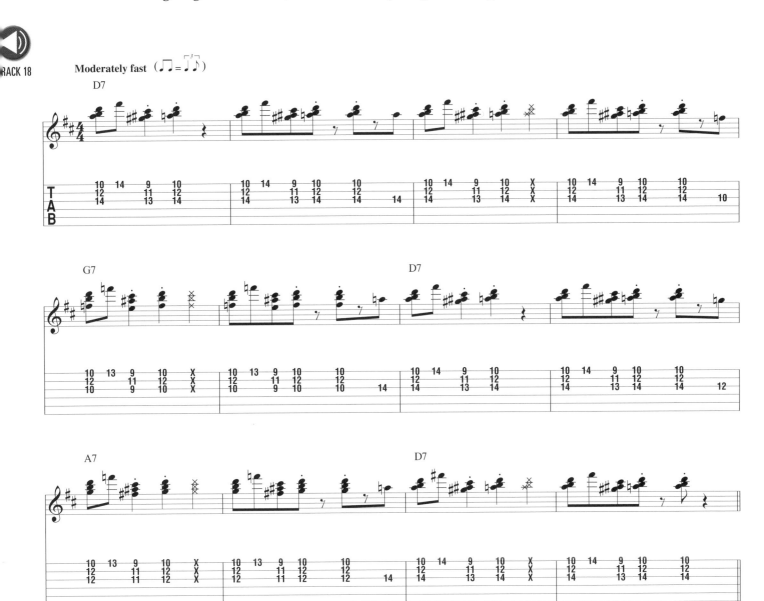

ADDING CHROMATICS

Breaking Away from the Pentatonic Box with a Few Jazz-Inspired Note Choices

This riff is another favorite idea of mine that makes use of chromatic notes to jazz up the blues a little. These types of lines sound equally at home in several different blues settings, and they're nice for adding a bit of sophistication, which helps to break up the standard blues guitar minor pentatonic vocabulary. You could even play this over a jazz blues and sound authentic, as it's reminiscent of something that Charlie Christian or Grant Green may have played, but it's been adopted by B.B. King and many others since.

As is typical of jazzier phrasing, we're playing constant eighth notes here. Working in the key of B♭, we begin with a three-note chromatic climb in ninth position: D♭ (minor 3rd)–D (major 3rd)–E♭ (4th) and continue back down to D♭. The logic of this move is immediately revealed on beat 3, where we arrive back at the major 3rd (D). This "encircling" of the major 3rd (in this case, E♭–D♭–D) is a staple of jazz and jazz blues, and I find myself often making use of the concept in my playing. From there, I slide down string 2, from B♭ to F, which is a technique used by many blues players. A jazz teacher would likely tell you not to do this, but it's a staple of the blues guitar style—most likely a product of the habit many blues guitarists have of staying mostly on the top three strings after leaving "root" position. Nevertheless, it's an effective blues sound that we all gravitate toward and copy.

Once in the root position (in this case, sixth position) for the F note, I begin the next phase of the riff by continuing down the scale to E♭ on string 3. Measure 2 begins with a grace-note hammer-on from D♭ to D (minor 3rd to major 3rd)—one of the most common moves in all of blues guitar. Next, I descend through the tonic (B♭) on string 4 and the 5th (F) on string 5, moving down in half steps to the E♭ on beat 3. It's worth comparing beats 3–4 of measure 1 with beats 1–2 of measure 2 to see how similar they are. With the exception of the last note (F♭), the latter is simply the former played an octave lower. We finish up measure 2 by surrounding the major 3rd yet again, only this time we make use of the 2nd (C) on string 6 as opposed to the minor 3rd (as before)—although we do slide into the major 3rd (D) from the minor 3rd (C♯/D♭) on beat 4. This major 3rd is followed by the tonic (B♭) on string 4, which is one of the most common endings in jazz and blues riffs alike.

This riff is a prime example of a phrase that uses major 3rds in a blues context while still sounding nice and bluesy. Many players shy away from learning jazz-inspired ideas because they feel that jazz sounds too "outside" and won't work in a 12-bar format. However, that's not the case, as this riff demonstrates. The effect can be a bit more subtle, while still providing a nice break from the standard pentatonic blues box.

GETTIN' DOWN AND FUNKIN' IT UP
Two Ideas to Help Your Blues Get a Little Ruder

In this lesson, we'll look at a funky blues riff in B♭ that makes use of a few specific devices that can be put to use a number of ways—namely, *sliding double stops* and *rapid, descending pull-offs*. Both of these techniques are common to funkier styles, but we can certainly find ways to incorporate them into bluesier things, as well. Nearly the entire lick is played out of the B♭ blues box in sixth position, which should be familiar to almost everyone. Just in case, though, here's the B♭ blues scale in this box:

B♭ Blues Scale

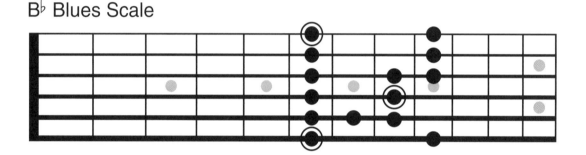

We start off on beats 1 and 2 by jumbling a few notes (A♭, F, and B♭) around to create a somewhat angular melody that gets your attention. At beat 3, begin phrasing in double stops, sliding and pulling off a major 3rd shape on strings 3 and 2 that makes use of the ♭5th blues note (F♭). Notice also that there's one note here—a product of our parallel double-stop phrasing—that's not found in the B♭ blues scale: the 6th (G). Although this sound is extremely common in blues, rock, country, and other styles, it's not one that fits neatly into one scale. It could be described as a blues/Dorian hybrid scale, but most players only make use of this concept on the upper strings. Here's a fingering for this hybrid B♭ blues scale that players often work out of:

B♭ Blues Scale/Dorian Hybrid

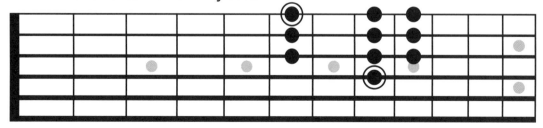

Measure 2 of our riff begins with our next topic of discussion: rapid, descending pull-offs. This is a technique that's been used by many bluesmen, including Stevie Ray Vaughan, Johnny Winter, Buddy Guy, and plenty of others. The effect is really more important than the actual notes, which just run straight down the B♭ minor pentatonic scale after the quarter-step bend of the ♭3rd, D♭. As a variation on this lick, you can get by without even picking the fifth string; Stevie Ray would do this a lot. Instead, you would just pick the B♭ note on string 4, pull-off to A♭, then hammer down on the fifth-string F note and pull off to E♭.

Another interesting thing that happens here is the rhythmic effect. Notice that, when taken with the quarter-step bend of the D♭ note, this little lick takes up the space of three eighth notes. So, when you repeat it without a pause, as we do here, the riff begins the next time on an upbeat. You could continue repeating this riff over and over if you'd like, creating an on-the-beat/off-the-beat feel that builds tension that wants to be released.

After we play the rapid pull-off lick a second time, we take our only step out of the blues box to reach down for the ♭3rd (D♭) at fret 4 on string 5. We slide this note up a half step, to the major 3rd (D), and finish off with the root (B♭) on string 4. This minor 3rd–major 3rd–root move is a very common way to wrap up phrases in jazz, as well as in blues and country.

As mentioned earlier, each one of these ideas can be exploited in different ways. For instance, try moving the sliding double-stop lick on beat 3 of measure 1 up a string set, to strings 2 and 1. The same thing can be done with the rapid-fire pull-off lick. You can come up with dozens of more useable licks by thinking this way.

TRACK 20

DEEP POCKETS
Laying Down a Serious Groove

This lesson is all about laying down a slinky soul/jazz funk groove. It's tons of fun to play on this type of laid-back, '60s-style, bluesy funk rhythm. Sure, it's great to whip out fancy solos too, but there's a real unsung joy in sitting back and just grooving with the rhythm section. Bassists and drummers are always keen to this, and it's something that we guitarists should definitely experience more of.

The 12-bar riff here is crafted from the classic call-and-response method of playing a common pentatonic riff and answering with chord accents. In our case, we're in B♭, and the riff is drawn from the B♭ minor pentatonic scale, even though we're playing dominant B♭ chords. That is part of this riff's allure: the tension created by this dual tonality.

For the B♭ chords, we're alternating low B♭ root notes with chord stabs (B♭7 and E♭) on strings 4–2. In typical blues fashion, we're hammering from the minor 3rd (D♭) to the major 3rd (D) of the B♭7 chord for some extra grease. Additionally, we add a little hook by deliberately sliding the B♭7 chord fragment down a half step and back up.

For the E♭9 change (the IV chord), we're strumming a popular voicing with its root on the fifth string and making use of *scratch rhythm*—lightly touching the strings and strumming to produce a dead, scratchy tone—to generate rhythmic interest. We apply the chromatic half-step sliding trick to this chord, as well, which further reinforces the hook.

Instead of moving to the V chord, which would be F, we get the listener's attention by moving to the ♭III chord (D♭7) for all of measure 9. We then descend chromatically in measure 10 through C7 and B7 (each lasting two beats) to land back at B♭7 in measure 11. All three of these dominant chords (D♭7, C7, and B7) are treated to the same minor 3rd-to-major 3rd hammer-on move that is used on our B♭7 chord. Notice that we leave the texture here sparse and open, further contrasting this section with the rest of the riff's busy nature. As is typical with this kind of blues riff, there is no turnaround; it ends just as it began.

Be sure to check out the subtleties in this riff, including the staccato chords (usually on beat 2) and the minor 3rd-to-major 3rd hammer-ons. These devices are really important and would be severely missed if they disappeared. This type of riff structure can be heard in countless blues tunes, including "The Thrill Is Gone," "Mary Had a Little Lamb," and "Hideaway" to name but a few. The next time you get together to jam, try pulling out one of these riffs and concentrate on doing nothing but sinking deep into the pocket.

Moderately slow

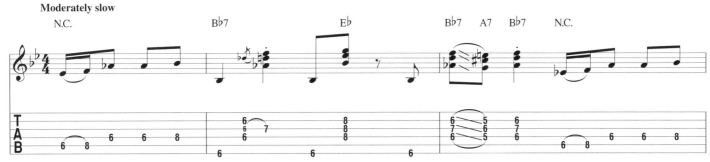

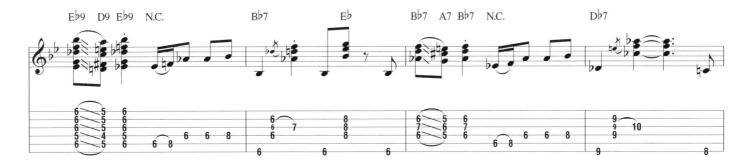

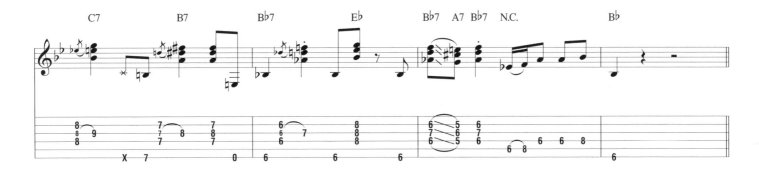

MIXIN' IT UP AND KEEPING IT FRESH

Using Imitation and Contrasting Rhythms to Liven Up the Slow Shuffle

In this lesson, we're going to look at a Charlie Parker blues riff that Herb Ellis quoted on our *Conversations in Swing* album. The idea of quoting is a common practice in jazz and blues, and it's a good opportunity to pay homage to your influences while also assimilating their sound into yours through your own interpretation. Every player has his own sonic fingerprint, and therefore everyone sounds different—even when playing the same thing. Couple this with the fact that each player also has his own approach to technique, tone, etc., and it's quite easy to end up with something that sounds unique to you.

The following example is a slow blues in the key of B♭ and starts with a very standard, major-pentatonic pickup lick that opens quite a few B.B. King solos. When we reach the high B♭ on string 1, we immediately jump back down to the low octave and finish the phrase off with another minor 3rd-to-major 3rd hammer-on. The rhythm is a big part of this phrase's appeal, and the syncopated ending is especially funky. On beat 4, we employ another common rhythmic trick in jazz/blues: playing straight 16th notes over a slow shuffle feel. This is a really nice way to shake things up and keep it fresh. The choice of the major 7th (A) as an approach tone to the root B♭ is also striking. After a quick F note on the downbeat of measure 2, we resolve to E♭ for the "quick change" IV chord. The end of measure 2 features the same pickup riff from the beginning to lead back to the I chord in measure 3. The 16th-note lick at the end of measure 3 is a great example of imitation, this time approaching the 5th (F) from a half step below, the dissonant ♭5th (E/F♭). There are two types of imitation: rhythmic and melodic. This lick is a combination of both.

The imitation continues into measure 4, where the lopsided shuffled rhythm from beat 1 of measure 2 is used for the D (approached from a half step below) and A♭ notes, which outline the B♭7 harmony via the 3rd and ♭7th, respectively. Beats 3 and 4 of measure 4 sound particularly jazzy and again make use of the 16th-note rhythm (with a quick 32nd-note flourish, as well). This line begins by nicking both the ♭9th (B/C♭) and ♯9th (D♭/C♯) and resolving to the root (B♭) with a quick pull-and-slide maneuver. Without stopping, it continues descending to the ♭7th (A♭), and then on down chromatically through G, G♭, F, and F♭. This puts us in a perfect position to resolve to E♭ for the arrival of the IV chord in measure 5. Once there, we work out of the box position at fret 6 with a combination of notes from the B♭ blues scale (B♭–D♭–E♭–E–F–A♭) and B♭ Dorian mode (B♭–C–D♭–E♭–F–G–A♭). For the organ-like double-stop riff on beats 3–4, remain in sixth position and keep your third finger on the B♭ note, flattening it out for the E♭/G dyad and barring your first finger for the D♭/F dyad. After a quick, passing A♭/D dyad (suggesting a brief B♭7), we come to rest on a rootless E♭9 chord voicing in measure 6.

Try playing around with these ideas in your own lines—especially mixing up the rhythms, melodic/rhythmic imitation, and the ♭9th/♯9th motif in measure 4. There's quite a bit packed into these six measures. I sometimes use this riff as the start of a verse when I play "Blues for Herb Ellis" live.

TRACK 22

GOING OUT, IN STYLE

Using Jazzy Double Stops and Chords to Close Out a Blues

Here is a nice, little ending riff in the key of G that you can use when you want to mix a little blues with your jazz. This two-measure phrase begins in measure 11 of the 12-bar form, and you want to make sure everyone in the band knows that you're ending the tune! The implied chords in measure 1 are G, G7/B, C, and C#°7. These chords create an ascending bass line that the bass player will undoubtedly play. The implied bass line would wrap up on beat 1 of measure 2 (i.e., with the G/D chord), and on beat 2, we cap the riff off with a classic, chromatic ♭II–I chord move—in this case, A♭13 to G13.

We kick things off with a blues-certified T-Bone Walker move. We're playing the 6th (E) and ♭3rd (B♭) on strings 2 and 1, respectively, and giving them a slight quarter-step bend. Try fingering these notes with fingers 2 and 3 or fingers 3 and 4 to see what feels more comfortable. Beat 2 continues with a G–F–D triplet that moves straight down the G minor pentatonic scale. On beat 3, we're sliding up into a typical 5th/♭7th (D/F) blues double stop to begin a little two-beat lick that pivots off the G note on string 4. Notice the two grace-note slides—one up a half step (beat 3) and one down a half step (beat 4). Descending grace-note slides (as on beat 4) aren't quite as common as ascending ones, but they should be! They're extremely expressive and can really add a sassy quality to a line.

We begin the second measure in typical blues fashion, hammering from the minor 3rd to the major 3rd of the tonic (G) chord. On beat 2, we join the rhythm section with a chord hit to wrap things up. For the A♭13 voicing, notice that you need to mute string 5 so you're able to strum through all six strings, which is accomplished by letting one (or both) of the fingers fretting the adjacent strings lightly touch the fifth string. Then, we simply move the same, exact chord voicing down a half step, to G13. This chromatic move on beat 2 of the final measure of the 12-bar form is one of the most common endings in all of blues. The other most common ending is the opposite: moving up to the tonic from a half step below, which, in this case, would be F#13 to G13.

To put the icing on the cake, we slowly and deliberately slide up the fourth string to ninth position and brush through a G9#11 voicing. This is a *rootless voicing* (it doesn't contain a G note), which is quite common in jazz guitar. The #11th note on top (C#) kind of tickles the ear and, since it sounds unresolved, leaves the listener wanting to hear more.

Although this ending is mostly used in slower-tempo blues tunes, you could play it in mid-tempo grooves, as well. Remember, nailing the chord hits on beat 2 of the second measure is the most important thing. There are a million ways to get there from the beginning, but if you miss those hits, you miss a big opportunity to sound like a seasoned pro.

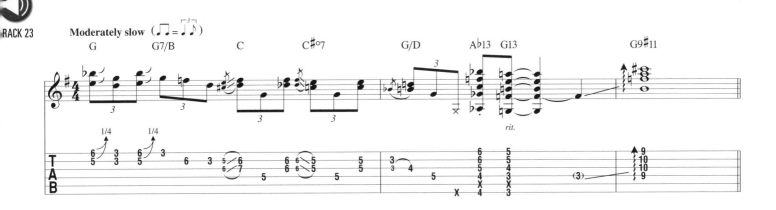

SET IT UP, BASIE-STYLE!
A Classic-Sounding, Versatile Intro

This lesson explores a nice intro riff that you can use in a variety of ways. It'll work in front of a 12-bar blues, a ballad, a swing tune, and more. It has an old-time jazzy sound to it that harkens back to the swing bands of the '30s and '40s, such as Count Basie or Duke Ellington. If you want to be a working blues/jazz player, it's important to have a large stock of intros and outros at the ready. You never know when you'll be called on to "set up" a tune, so it helps to be prepared!

The basis for this intro is a I–VI–ii–V progression in the key of Bb. I–VI–ii–V is one of the most popular progressions in jazz and swing music, and you'll see it all the time in standard tunes. In Bb, these basic chords would be Bb (I), G (VI), Cm (ii), and F (V). Of course, jazz has a knack for sophisticated harmonies, so things are rarely that simple, as we'll soon see. We begin with a Bb6 chord in first inversion, which means that the 3rd of the chord (D) is on the bottom, instead of the root (Bb). So, the chord is voiced, low to high: D (3rd)–Bb (root)–F (5th)–G (6th).

The next chord is a bit trickier. Normally, in this progression, we'd see a G7 chord here. However, we want to create a chromatically descending bass line from the D note to the root of the ii chord, C, so we need a Db as the next bass note. Generally speaking, whenever you have a passing chromatic bass note, you can harmonize it with a diminished seventh chord, and that's what's been done here. It's not just a random diminished chord, though; it's actually functioning as a substitute for an *altered* G7 chord—altered meaning that the 5th and/or the 9th have been raised or lowered by a half step. If we look at each note as it relates to G, we see that Db is the b5th, Cbb (or A#) is the #9th, and Fb (or E) is the 13th.

In measure 2, we have a standard Cm7 voicing: root (C)–b7th (Bb)–b3rd (Eb)–5th (G), low to high. This measure is fleshed out a bit in chord-melody style with an ascending line on string 2 from the Bb major scale. On beat 3, we have a quick, rootless Cm9 voicing (the ii chord) on the top four strings that's followed by the V chord, F13b9. This is another rootless voicing, arranged as follows: 3rd (A)–b7th (Eb)–b9th (Gb)–13th (D), low to high. Notice the relationship between this chord and the Cm9 voicing. Two tones stay the same—Eb and the high D—which results in smooth voice leading.

After repeating measure 1's chords in measure 3, we mix it up in measure 4 with a chromatic single-note riff over the Cm7 chord, played in eighth position. This leads nicely to the rootless F13 chord on beat 3. Note that the only difference between this chord and the F13♭9 chord in measure 2 is that the G note has not been raised a half step here. We close it all out with a B♭6 chord on the downbeat of measure 5. This chord could be replaced with other types of B♭ chords, depending on the song. For example, if it were a 12-bar blues, you might play B♭7 or B♭9. If it were a ballad, you might play B♭maj7 or B♭maj13, etc.

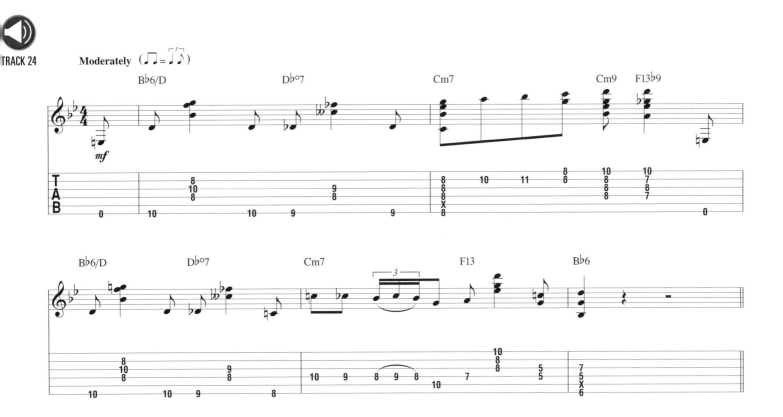

ROLLIN' THROUGH THE CHANGES
A Nice Arpeggio-Pattern Accompaniment

In this lesson, we'll look at a cool arpeggio riff from the '40s that was originally played on piano. It works great for guitar, however, as we'll soon see. An *arpeggio* is simply the notes of a chord played separately, as a melody, rather than simultaneously. Arpeggios can be created by picking the notes of a chord one at a time, so that all the notes ring together, or they can be created by playing the notes one at a time, as in a lick or riff. We've done the latter here.

This riff is designed to be played over a 12-bar blues, and I've demonstrated how it sounds over the I and IV chords in a blues in the key of A: A7 and D7, respectively. The default harmony for each chord in a 12-bar blues is the dominant seventh chord, which contains the root, 3rd, 5th, and ♭7th. You can play many arpeggio patterns using these four notes, and many classic blues bass lines have been built this way. In this riff, however, we're going to spice it up with a few other tricks. Rhythmically, we're playing straight triplets throughout this entire riff.

After the open low-E string pickup note, we begin in fourth position with our second finger on the low, tonic A note. Then, we climb straight up an A7 arpeggio: A–C♯–E–G–A. But since this is only five notes, and we need six to complete our two-beat triplet pattern, we need one more on top. The solution is the hip 9th (B) tone, which is played by quickly shifting up two frets and back. Next, we continue descending through A, G, and E on beat 3. On beat 4, though, we switch gears and ascend C (♭3rd), C♯ (3rd), and E (5th) to round out the one-measure pattern. This ♭3rd–3rd–5th sequence is a classic move in blues and jazz. Measures 2, 3, and 4 are essentially the same, but we've added a few grace-note slides for a little character.

Now comes the easy part: For the IV chord in measures 5–6, you just move the entire pattern over a string set, starting on string 5 (instead of string 6). Since we're not making use of that pesky B string, all the fingerings are exactly the same. Notice that slight variation on beat 3 of measure 6, ornamenting the D note with a quick hammer-on to E—just a little twist on the repeating pattern. In measures 7–8, we finish up with a return to the I chord and the original riff in A.

This riff could be transposed to the V chord, E, if you'd like. In that case, you'd simply take the riff from measures 5–6 and move it up two frets. However, I generally prefer to break the pattern there, usually by moving into an ascending line of B–C#–D–D# in measure 9 and a descending line of E–D–C#–B in measure 10 (all quarter notes or double-picked as eighth notes). You could then resume the A7 version of the riff for measures 11–12 or go into one of many turnaround licks. Although this riff is fairly busy, it provides a nice lift behind a soloist and can help elevate the intensity.

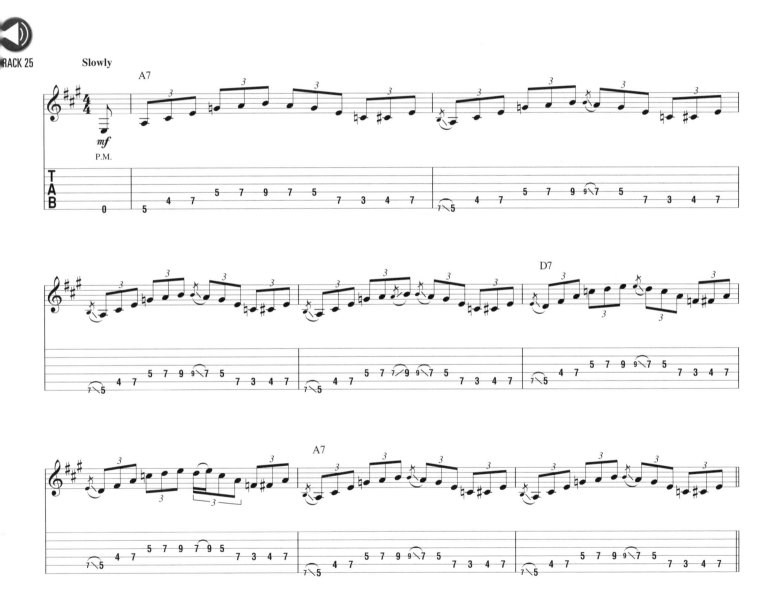

DOUBLE- AND TRIPLE-STOP RUN

Break up the Sound of a Single-Note Solo with This Phrase

The following example is a great riff to use in a sparse blues setting—a duo or trio, especially—when there's not of lot going on beneath your solo. When you're playing with, say, just a bassist and a drummer, it's nice to know a bunch of these kinds of licks that contain a mixture of single notes, double stops, triple stops, and/or full chords to help fill out the sound and keep it interesting.

This one's in the key of B♭ and begins on beat 3 of measure 3 of a 12-bar blues. We start with a cool double-stop maneuver that takes a major 3rd interval—B♭ on string 2 and D on string 1—and slides it down a whole step, to A♭/C. This simple trick is a great way to easily imply a dominant-ninth sound, since A♭ is the ♭7th of B♭, and C is the 9th. Make sure to use your second finger on string 2 and your first finger on string 1 for these double stops, as this will put you in perfect position for the rest of the phrase. On beat 4, you just need to lift your first finger and add your third finger to the F note on string 3, rounding out the measure with your first finger on the low B♭.

At the beginning of the next measure, we have a classic blues double-stop move on strings 3 and 2. For the first dyad, E♭/G, you can either remain in eighth position and barre your first finger (which was just fretting the B♭ note on string 4) or you can quickly shift to sixth position and barre it with your third finger. You'll need to be in sixth position for the D/F dyad (and the bluesy C♯-to-D hammer-on) that follows anyway, so go with whichever way feels best to you. On beat 2, we begin a move that's similar to the opening notes. Here, though, we're down an octave and moving chromatically to include the A/C♯ dyad in between the B♭/D and A♭/C double stops. After we reach the A♭/C dyad, we quickly jab a low B♭ on string 6 with finger 2 (or, alternatively, with your thumb).

This is followed on beat 4 with the real spice of the riff: a half-step slide up to a Bb7#5 chord, using our first finger for the Ab note on string 4 and barring our third (or possibly second, if you like) finger for the D and F# notes on strings 3 and 2, respectively. This is what's known as an *altered dominant* chord because the 5th of the chord (F, in this case) has been altered (raised a half step). Altered dominants are all over the place in jazz and jazzier blues tunes, and this, measure 4 of a 12-bar form, is one of the most common places to find them. It's a great way to lead to the IV chord, because altered dominant chords really sound as though they need to resolve. In this case, that resolution occurs immediately by sliding into a rootless Eb9 chord from a half step below. Note that the Eb9 triple stop, G–Db–F (3rd, b7th, and 9th of Eb) is only a half step below the Bb7#5 triple stop: Ab–D–F# (b7th, 3rd, and #5th of Bb). It sounds great, and it's fun to play.

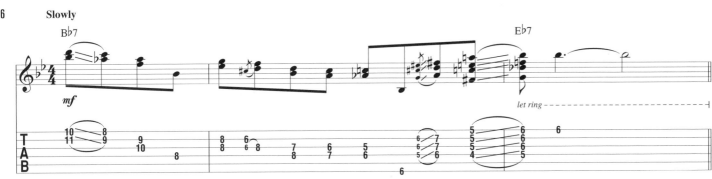

RAKIN' AND SLURRIN', PIANO-STYLE
Emulating a Piano Shuffle Riff

In this lesson, we're going to learn a great 12-bar riff that emulates the sound of a piano. It's full of double stops, triple stops, rakes, and slurs, and it's not all that easy to perform. You'd hear Ray Charles play this type of thing a lot, and it's a common boogie/shuffle sound on piano. It's not nearly as common on guitar, though, because it doesn't lie quite as nicely under the fingers as most riffs, but that's no reason not to learn it! Let's dig in.

This one's in the key of G, and we begin with a pickup phrase that's nearly a whole measure long. After a typical double-stop move of C/E to Bb/D, the lower of which is hammered to B, we use a reverse rake down to the fifth string. To perform this maneuver, release the pressure from the frets, but maintain contact with the strings, dragging the pick from string 2 to string 5 in a relaxed motion. You shouldn't hear any real discernible notes; the effect is more of a "blur." On beat 4, we play a C5 power chord in anticipation of the true target: a first-inversion G chord that is voiced as a B/G dyad, which is allowed to sustain over the bar line to the "true" first measure of the 12-bar form.

We begin measure 1 with a G major barre chord, hammering from the minor 3rd to the major 3rd on beat 2. What follows is a little chord riff that is played on strings 5–3 and makes use of first-inversion triads. On beat 3, we have a C triad (E–G–C) that's followed by a Dm triad (F–A–D) and a return back to the C on beat 4. The fingering of these triads can be tricky, as you have to shift smoothly and quickly to make it happen. That riff leads nicely back to the G chord on beat 1 of measure 2. After the downbeat in measure 4, we shift up to eighth position to play almost the same riff, transposed up for the IV (C7) chord. The only real difference is that, instead of playing full, three-note triads for the neighboring chord riff, we play 6th intervals, with string 4 muted in between.

We return to the G7 version of the riff on beat 2 of measure 6. In measure 8, we take a detour to F7 and E7 on beat 2. There are a few things to note here. First, harmonically speaking, the E7 is the VI chord in the key of G. (The F7 is simply a chromatic approach chord.) In a jazz blues, measure 8 (or the second half of measure 8, as is the case here) will often move to the VI chord in preparation for a ii–V chord progression in measures 9–10. The other interesting thing about these voicings is that they're rootless. Instead of having the root on string 5, we're playing the 5th on string 6 and muting string 5. When taken with the next two chords—Bbm7 (a chromatic approach chord) and Am7 (the ii chord)—the bass line moves chromatically: C–B–Bb–A. Pretty nifty, huh? Use your second finger for the bass note in all four of these chords. For F7 and E7, use fingers 1 and 3 on strings 4 and 3, respectively, and for Bbm7 and Am7, flatten out your third finger to barre strings 4–2. Have fun with this one, and make sure to strive for that relaxed, easy-going feel, just like those pianists get.

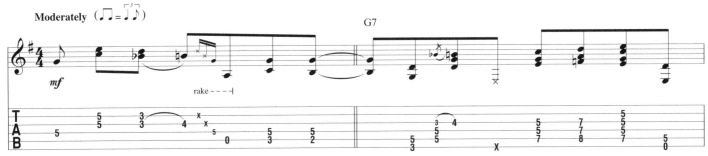

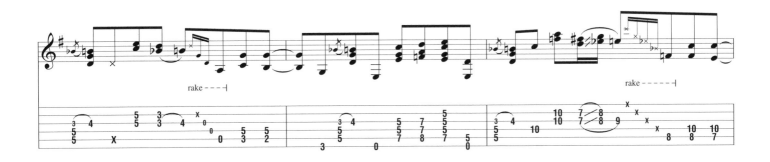

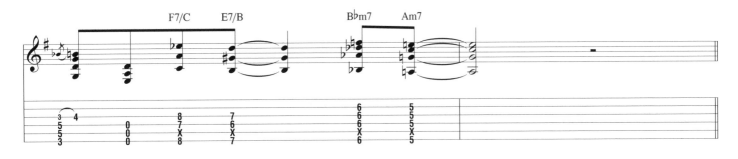

QUESTION-AND-ANSWER RIFF
A Classic I–vi–ii–V Riff in the Key of B♭

This lesson takes a look at a tune of mine called "Skippy's Dream," from my Duke Robillard Jazz Trio CD *Wobble Walkin'*. The following example is definitely more on the jazz side of things, but there's plenty of room for this type of thing in the blues, as well. This riff is based on a I–vi–ii–V progression in B♭: B♭–Gm7–Cm7–F7. As I've mentioned before, the I–vi–ii–V progression is everywhere in jazz, as well as in older blues tunes. This riff is set up in a question-and-answer format. In other words, the guitar plays a riff in measures 1 and 2, and then another instrument (bass, piano, etc.) "answers" in measures 3–4. Let's take a look at the riff.

After an F pickup note, we begin with a concept called *encircling*. Our target note is the B♭ on string 1, but instead of just playing F to Bb, which is a bit predictable, we "encircle" the B♭ by first playing A and C. Encircling is something you'll hear all the time in jazz solos. When we do reach the B♭ on beat 2, we "ornament" it with a quick pull-off to the B♭ note and then continue to descend straight down a B♭ major arpeggio. Notice how the D and B♭ notes on beat 3 also fit the Gm7 chord, where they act as the 5th and ♭3rd, respectively. In fact, almost any line you play over a I chord (B♭, in this case) will work over the vi chord (Gm7, in this case), as well.

Continuing on to the ii chord (Cm7) in measure 2, we approach its 5th (G) with a half-step slide from below—another extremely common jazz device that's also heard in blues, as well. From the G note, we continue down a Cm arpeggio and decorate the root note, C, with a quick, 16th-note triplet hammer/pull to E♭ and back, following it with the ♭7th (B♭) on the "and" of beat 2. In another classic jazz move, this ♭7th resolves down by a half step, to the 3rd of a dominant chord (in this case, the V chord, F7). From there, we proceed with a staple of the bebop vocabulary, leaping up to the ♭9th (G♭) of F7 and descending down the notes F and E♭ to resolve on the 3rd (D) of the I (B♭) chord in measure 3. You'll hear this lick in more jazz solos than you can shake a stick at.

Measures 5–6 are nearly identical to measures 1–2, with the only exception being the variation at the end of measure 6, over the F7 chord. Instead of the altered phrase of measure 2, after the A note, we dip down to F and jump back up to A, which resolves up a half step to a syncopated tonic note (B♭). This question-and-answer format can be a lot of fun to work with, and it's a good way to practice the art of resolving your lines on a certain target beat.

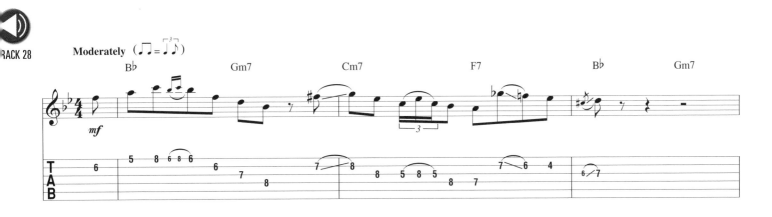

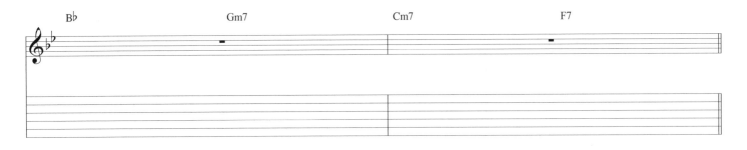

A WOBBLY BLUES RIFF
How the Dorian Mode Can Be Mixed with Other Tonalities in the Blues

The following example is the "head" from my tune "Wobble Walkin'," which is the title track from my 2012 album of the same name. It's in the key of C minor and features a few unusual harmonies for a blues tune. Let's take a look. (Note: On the audio, I'm playing just the melody, but you may want to play the chord changes to hear how the melody sounds against them.)

The backbone of this riff is a i–IV progression in C minor, shown here as Cm–F7. We begin with a pickup phrase in eighth position, from the C minor pentatonic scale, and hit a standard double-stop riff, F/A to E♭/G, on beat 1. The A note comes from the C Dorian mode, which is also suggested by the Cm–F7 chord progression. In fact, a minor tonic chord and a major (or dominant) IV chord (as opposed to the diatonic minor iv) is a classic example of the Dorian sound. On beat 2, we resolve the double-stop tension with a syncopated C–B♭–C triplet melody that swings heavily. At the end of measure 1, we begin to repeat the phrase, including the same pickup line (G–B♭–C), but vary the phrase's ending by reversing our approach, playing single notes first and ending with a syncopated triplet double stop.

Measure 3 is a repeat of measure 1, but things really take a turn in measure 4. Here, we have a G7♭5 chord, which is an altered dominant chord. After decorating the major 3rd (B) with all kinds of slippery legato moves and following it with the root (G) on string 5, we make a surprise leap up to an octave D♭ note for a real ear-grabber. This D♭ note is actually the ♭5th of the G7♭5 chord (G–B–D♭–F), so it does work with the underlying harmony. In measures 5–6, we pick things back up as if nothing funky had happened at all, repeating the material from measures 1–2. At measure 7, we begin to wrap it all up with a descending series of triplet arpeggios on strings 4–2 that follow the chord progression shown: Cm (i)–B♭m (♭vii)–A♭7 (♭VI)–G7 (V). (Though A♭7 and G7 are the chords, I'm only playing major triad arpeggios for each.) The B♭m is a surprise here, as you expect to hear the diatonic B♭ major chord. The V chord, G7, is extended to the beginning of measure 8, where it's altered to a G7♯5 chord (G–B–D♯–F), which is reflected in the melody, as I'm playing D♯ and B before resolving to the tonic note, C.

There are a few other things to take note of here. First is the articulation, which is a big part of the riff's appeal. Notice all the staccato marks (dots over/under certain notes). This means to play the notes short and clipped; you can clearly hear this on the audio. There's also a question-and-answer approach being used here; for example, the phrase in measure 1 asks a "question" that the similar phrase in measure 2 "answers." You could even extend this idea to a larger scale. For example, measures 1 and 2, taken together, ask a question that measures 3 and 4 answer. This concept of using similar phrases with different endings helps give a riff (or solo or head) a sense of cohesion and makes it easier to remember.

CLOSING TIME
An Ending Lick Packed with Flavor

Here's a great blues lick that I use all the time. It works well as an ending, when the band has stopped and everyone's waiting on you to bring it home. The lick's not too long, but it has a lot of cool things happening every step of the way. It's played in a free yet enthusiastic rhythm, so it's actually preferable to play this one solo. The lick is in the key of C, but since there are no open strings, you can easily move it to any key. Let's check it out.

Nearly the whole lick takes place in the eighth-position blues box. It starts with a nice, B.B.-sounding opening phrase from the C major pentatonic scale (C–D–E–G–A) that moves from G (5th) to A (6th) to C (root). Next, we hit a soaring bend from E♭ to F, which is from the C minor pentatonic scale (C–E♭–F–G–B♭). This major and minor scale mixing is a favorite sound of B.B., as well as one his idols, T-Bone Walker. Here, we begin our descent with a sweet half-step bend from E♭ to E, and then continue straight down the C minor pentatonic scale: C–B♭–G.

Moving down to the thicker G string, we slide the F note up a half step to the bluesy ♭5th (G♭), and then pull off from F to E♭, giving it a sassy half-step bend before resolving to the root, C, on string 4. These subtle bends and slides are so important in the blues and are responsible for turning an ordinary riff or lick into something that's full of character. Moving on, we leap down to the 5th (G) on string 5 and descend chromatically, G–G♭–F, which is right out of the C blues scale (C–E♭–F–G♭–G–B♭). We finish off with a quick hammer/pull (F–G–F) figure and whole-step slide down to the ♭3rd (E♭), "overshooting" the true target note, E (the major 3rd), which we quickly resolve to. To cap it all off, hold the E note and add B♭, D, and G above it to form a rootless C9 chord. This is the voicing that T-Bone made famous, and I like to call it the "inside" ninth chord because it sits on the inside string set. Have fun with this one, and be sure to milk every note for all it's worth!

TRACK 30

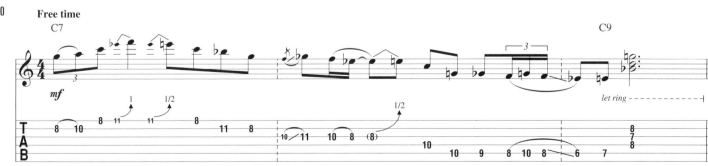

GUITAR NOTATION LEGEND

Guitar music can be notated three different ways: on a *musical staff*, in *tablature*, and in *rhythm slashes*.

RHYTHM SLASHES are written above the staff. Strum chords in the rhythm indicated. Use the chord diagrams found at the top of the first page of the transcription for the appropriate chord voicings. Round noteheads indicate single notes.

THE MUSICAL STAFF shows pitches and rhythms and is divided by bar lines into measures. Pitches are named after the first seven letters of the alphabet.

TABLATURE graphically represents the guitar fingerboard. Each horizontal line represents a string, and each number represents a fret.

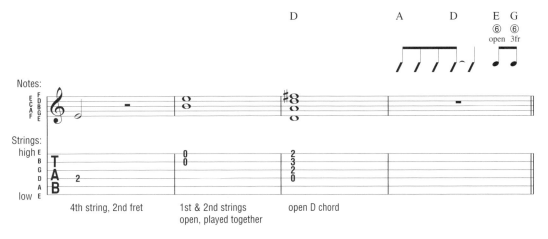

4th string, 2nd fret · 1st & 2nd strings open, played together · open D chord

Definitions for Special Guitar Notation

HALF-STEP BEND: Strike the note and bend up 1/2 step.

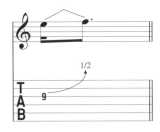

WHOLE-STEP BEND: Strike the note and bend up one step.

GRACE NOTE BEND: Strike the note and immediately bend up as indicated.

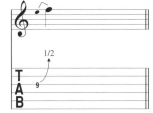

SLIGHT (MICROTONE) BEND: Strike the note and bend up 1/4 step.

BEND AND RELEASE: Strike the note and bend up as indicated, then release back to the original note. Only the first note is struck.

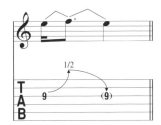

PRE-BEND: Bend the note as indicated, then strike it.

PRE-BEND AND RELEASE: Bend the note as indicated. Strike it and release the bend back to the original note.

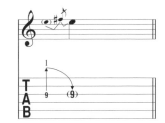

UNISON BEND: Strike the two notes simultaneously and bend the lower note up to the pitch of the higher.

VIBRATO: The string is vibrated by rapidly bending and releasing the note with the fretting hand.

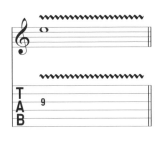

WIDE VIBRATO: The pitch is varied to a greater degree by vibrating with the fretting hand.

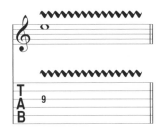

HAMMER-ON: Strike the first (lower) note with one finger, then sound the higher note (on the same string) with another finger by fretting it without picking.

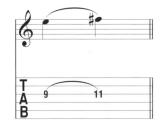

PULL-OFF: Place both fingers on the notes to be sounded. Strike the first note and without picking, pull the finger off to sound the second (lower) note.

LEGATO SLIDE: Strike the first note and then slide the same fret-hand finger up or down to the second note. The second note is not struck.

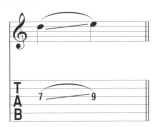

SHIFT SLIDE: Same as legato slide, except the second note is struck.

TRILL: Very rapidly alternate between the notes indicated by continuously hammering on and pulling off.

TAPPING: Hammer ("tap") the fret indicated with the pick-hand index or middle finger and pull off to the note fretted by the fret hand.

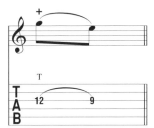

NATURAL HARMONIC: Strike the note while the fret-hand lightly touches the string directly over the fret indicated.

Harm.

PINCH HARMONIC: The note is fretted normally and a harmonic is produced by adding the edge of the thumb or the tip of the index finger of the pick hand to the normal pick attack.

P.H.

HARP HARMONIC: The note is fretted normally and a harmonic is produced by gently resting the pick hand's index finger directly above the indicated fret (in parentheses) while the pick hand's thumb or pick assists by plucking the appropriate string.

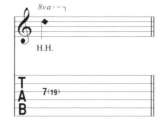
H.H.

PICK SCRAPE: The edge of the pick is rubbed down (or up) the string, producing a scratchy sound.

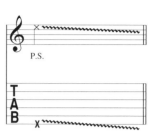
P.S.

MUFFLED STRINGS: A percussive sound is produced by laying the fret hand across the string(s) without depressing, and striking them with the pick hand.

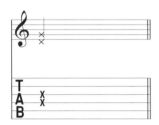

PALM MUTING: The note is partially muted by the pick hand lightly touching the string(s) just before the bridge.

P.M.

RAKE: Drag the pick across the strings indicated with a single motion.

rake

TREMOLO PICKING: The note is picked as rapidly and continuously as possible.

ARPEGGIATE: Play the notes of the chord indicated by quickly rolling them from bottom to top.

VIBRATO BAR DIVE AND RETURN: The pitch of the note or chord is dropped a specified number of steps (in rhythm), then returned to the original pitch.

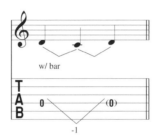
w/ bar

VIBRATO BAR SCOOP: Depress the bar just before striking the note, then quickly release the bar.

w/ bar

VIBRATO BAR DIP: Strike the note and then immediately drop a specified number of steps, then release back to the original pitch.

w/ bar

Additional Musical Definitions

(accent)	• Accentuate note (play it louder).	
(accent)	• Accentuate note with great intensity.	
(staccato)	• Play the note short.	
⊓	• Downstroke	
∨	• Upstroke	
D.S. al Coda	• Go back to the sign (𝄉), then play until the measure marked "*To Coda*," then skip to the section labelled "**Coda**."	
D.C. al Fine	• Go back to the beginning of the song and play until the measure marked "*Fine*" (end).	

Rhy. Fig. • Label used to recall a recurring accompaniment pattern (usually chordal).

Riff • Label used to recall composed, melodic lines (usually single notes) which recur.

Fill • Label used to identify a brief melodic figure which is to be inserted into the arrangement.

Rhy. Fill • A chordal version of a Fill.

tacet • Instrument is silent (drops out).

• Repeat measures between signs.

• When a repeated section has different endings, play the first ending only the first time and the second ending only the second time.

NOTE: Tablature numbers in parentheses mean:
1. The note is being sustained over a system (note in standard notation is tied), or
2. The note is sustained, but a new articulation (such as a hammer-on, pull-off, slide or vibrato) begins, or
3. The note is a barely audible "ghost" note (note in standard notation is also in parentheses).

Get Better at Guitar

...with these Great Guitar Instruction Books from Hal Leonard!

101 GUITAR TIPS
INCLUDES TAB

STUFF ALL THE PROS KNOW AND USE

by Adam St. James

This book contains invaluable guidance on everything from scales and music theory to truss rod adjustments, proper recording studio set-ups, and much more. The book also features snippets of advice from some of the most celebrated guitarists and producers in the music business, including B.B. King, Steve Vai, Joe Satriani, Warren Haynes, Laurence Juber, Pete Anderson, Tom Dowd and others, culled from the author's hundreds of interviews.

00695737 Book/CD Pack..........................$16.95

AMAZING PHRASING
INCLUDES TAB

50 WAYS TO IMPROVE YOUR IMPROVISATIONAL SKILLS

by Tom Kolb

This book/CD pack explores all the main components necessary for crafting well-balanced rhythmic and melodic phrases. It also explains how these phrases are put together to form cohesive solos. Many styles are covered – rock, blues, jazz, fusion, country, Latin, funk and more – and all of the concepts are backed up with musical examples. The companion CD contains 89 demos for listening, and most tracks feature full-band backing.

00695583 Book/CD Pack..........................$19.95

BLUES YOU CAN USE
INCLUDES TAB

by John Ganapes

A comprehensive source designed to help guitarists develop both lead and rhythm playing. Covers: Texas, Delta, R&B, early rock and roll, gospel, blues/rock and more. Includes: 21 complete solos • chord progressions and riffs • turnarounds • moveable scales and more. CD features leads and full band backing.

00695007 Book/CD Pack..........................$19.95

FRETBOARD MASTERY
INCLUDES TAB

by Troy Stetina

Untangle the mysterious regions of the guitar fretboard and unlock your potential. *Fretboard Mastery* familiarizes you with all the shapes you need to know by applying them in real musical examples, thereby reinforcing and reaffirming your newfound knowledge. The result is a much higher level of comprehension and retention.

00695331 Book/CD Pack..........................$19.95

FRETBOARD ROADMAPS – 2ND EDITION

ESSENTIAL GUITAR PATTERNS THAT ALL THE PROS KNOW AND USE

by Fred Sokolow

The updated edition of this bestseller features more songs, updated lessons, and a full audio CD! Learn to play lead and rhythm anywhere on the fretboard, in any key; play a variety of lead guitar styles; play chords and progressions anywhere on the fretboard; expand your chord vocabulary; and learn to think musically – the way the pros do.

00695941 Book/CD Pack..........................$14.95

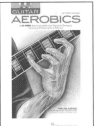

GUITAR AEROBICS
INCLUDES TAB

A 52-WEEK, ONE-LICK-PER-DAY WORKOUT PROGRAM FOR DEVELOPING, IMPROVING & MAINTAINING GUITAR TECHNIQUE

by Troy Nelson

From the former editor of *Guitar One* magazine, here is a daily dose of vitamins to keep your chops fine tuned! Musical styles include rock, blues, jazz, metal, country, and funk. Techniques taught include alternate picking, arpeggios, sweep picking, string skipping, legato, string bending, and rhythm guitar. These exercises will increase speed, and improve dexterity and pick- and fret-hand accuracy. The accompanying CD includes all 365 workout licks plus play-along grooves in every style at eight different metronome settings.

00695946 Book/CD Pack..........................$19.99

GUITAR CLUES
INCLUDES TAB

OPERATION PENTATONIC

by Greg Koch

Join renowned guitar master Greg Koch as he clues you in to a wide variety of fun and valuable pentatonic scale applications. Whether you're new to improvising or have been doing it for a while, this book/CD pack will provide loads of delicious licks and tricks that you can use right away, from volume swells and chicken pickin' to intervallic and chordal ideas. The CD includes 65 demo and play-along tracks.

00695827 Book/CD Pack..........................$19.95

INTRODUCTION TO GUITAR TONE & EFFECTS

by David M. Brewster

This book/CD pack teaches the basics of guitar tones and effects, with audio examples on CD. Readers will learn about: overdrive, distortion and fuzz • using equalizers • modulation effects • reverb and delay • multi-effect processors • and more.

00695766 Book/CD Pack..........................$14.99

PICTURE CHORD ENCYCLOPEDIA

This comprehensive guitar chord resource for all playing styles and levels features five voicings of 44 chord qualities for all twelve keys – 2,640 chords in all! For each, there is a clearly illustrated chord frame, as well as *an actual photo* of the chord being played! Includes info on basic fingering principles, open chords and barre chords, partial chords and broken-set forms, and more.

00695224..........................$19.95

SCALE CHORD RELATIONSHIPS
INCLUDES TAB

by Michael Mueller & Jeff Schroedl

This book teaches players how to determine which scales to play with which chords, so guitarists will never have to fear chord changes again! This book/CD pack explains how to: recognize keys • analyze chord progressions • use the modes • play over nondiatonic harmony • use harmonic and melodic minor scales • use symmetrical scales such as chromatic, whole-tone and diminished scales • incorporate exotic scales such as Hungarian major and Gypsy minor • and much more!

00695563 Book/CD Pack..........................$14.95

SPEED MECHANICS FOR LEAD GUITAR
INCLUDES TAB

Take your playing to the stratosphere with the most advanced lead book by this proven heavy metal author. *Speed Mechanics* is the ultimate technique book for developing the kind of speed and precision in today's explosive playing styles. Learn the fastest ways to achieve speed and control, secrets to make your practice time really count, and how to open your ears and make your musical ideas more solid and tangible. Packed with over 200 vicious exercises including Troy's scorching version of "Flight of the Bumblebee." Music and examples demonstrated on CD. 89-minute audio.

00699323 Book/CD Pack..........................$19.95

TOTAL ROCK GUITAR
INCLUDES TAB

A COMPLETE GUIDE TO LEARNING ROCK GUITAR

by Troy Stetina

This unique and comprehensive source for learning rock guitar is designed to develop both lead and rhythm playing. It covers: getting a tone that rocks • open chords, power chords and barre chords • riffs, scales and licks • string bending, strumming, palm muting, harmonics and alternate picking • all rock styles • and much more. The examples are in standard notation with chord grids and tab, and the CD includes full-band backing for all 22 songs.

00695246 Book/CD Pack..........................$19.99

MASTER THE *Blues*

With guitar instruction from Hal Leonard
All books include notes and tab.

Hal Leonard Guitar Method – Blues Guitar
by Greg Koch

The complete guide to learning blues guitar uses real blues songs to teach you the basics of rhythm and lead blues guitar in the style of B.B. King, Buddy Guy, Eric Clapton, and many others. Lessons include: 12-bar blues; chords, scales and licks; vibrato and string bending; riffs, turnarounds, and boogie patterns; and more!
00697326 Book/CD Pack $16.99

Blues Deluxe
by Dave Rubin

Not only does this deluxe edition provide accurate transcriptions of ten blues classics plus performance notes and artist bios, it also includes a CD with the *original Alligator Records recordings* of every song! Tunes: Are You Losing Your Mind? (Buddy Guy) • Don't Take Advantage of Me (Johnny Winter) • Gravel Road (Magic Slim) • Somebody Loan Me a Dime (Fenton Robinson) • and more.
00699918 Book/CD Pack.....................$24.99

Art of the Shuffle
by Dave Rubin

This method book explores shuffle, boogie and swing rhythms for guitar. Includes tab and notation, and covers Delta, country, Chicago, Kansas City, Texas, New Orleans, West Coast, and bebop blues. Also includes audio for demonstration of each style and to jam along with.
00695005 Book/CD Pack.....................$19.95

Power Trio Blues
by Dave Rubin

This book/CD pack details how to play electric guitar in a trio with bass and drums. Boogie, shuffle, and slow blues rhythms, licks, double stops, chords, and bass patterns are presented for full and exciting blues. A CD with the music examples performed by a smokin' power trio is included for play-along instruction and jamming.
00695028 Book/CD Pack.....................$19.99

100 Blues Lessons
Guitar Lesson Goldmine
by John Heussenstamm and Chad Johnson

A huge variety of blues guitar styles and techniques are covered, including: turnarounds, hammer-ons and pull-offs, slides, the blues scale, 12-bar blues, double stops, muting techniques, hybrid picking, fingerstyle blues, and much more!
00696452 Book/2-CD Pack.................$24.99

Electric Slide Guitar
by David Hamburger

This book/audio method explores the basic fundamentals of slide guitar: from selecting a slide and proper setup of the guitar, to open and standard tuning. Plenty of music examples are presented showing sample licks as well as backup/rhythm slide work. Each section also examines techniques and solos in the style of the best slide guitarists, including Duane Allman, Dave Hole, Ry Cooder, Bonnie Raitt, Muddy Waters, Johnny Winter and Elmore James.
00695022 Book/CD Pack....................$19.95

101 Must-Know Blues Licks
A Quick, Easy Reference for All Guitarists
by Wolf Marshall

Now you can add authentic blues feel and flavor to your playing! Here are 101 definitive licks – plus a demonstration CD – from every major blues guitar style, neatly organized into easy-to-use categories. They're all here, including Delta blues, jump blues, country blues, Memphis blues, Texas blues, West Coast blues, Chicago blues, and British blues.
00695318 Book/CD Pack.....................$17.95

Fretboard Roadmaps Blues Guitar
for Acoustic and Electric Guitar
by Fred Sokolow

These essential fretboard patterns are roadmaps that all great blues guitarists know and use. This book teaches how to: play lead and rhythm anywhere on the fretboard, in any key; play a variety of lead guitar styles; play chords and progressions anywhere on the fretboard, in any key; expand chord vocabulary; learn to think musically, the way the pros do.
00695350 Book/CD Pack.....................$14.95

The Road to Robert Johnson
The Genesis and Evolution of Blues in the Delta from the Late 1800s Through 1938
by Edward Komara

This book traces the development of the legendary Robert Johnson's music in light of the people and songs that directly and indirectly influenced him. It includes much information about life in the Delta from the late 1800s to Johnson's controversial death in 1938, and features fascinating historical photos, maps, musical examples, and much more.
00695388..$14.95

12-Bar Blues
by Dave Rubin

The term "12-bar blues" has become synonymous with blues music and is the basis for an incredible body of jazz, rock 'n' roll, and other forms of popular music. This book/CD pack is solely devoted to providing guitarists with all the technical tools necessary for playing 12-bar blues with authority. The CD includes 24 full-band tracks. Covers: boogie, shuffle, swing, riff, and jazzy blues progressions; Chicago, minor, slow, bebop, and other blues styles; soloing, intros, turnarounds, and more.
00695187 Book/CD Pack....................$18.99

Smokin' Blues Guitar
by Smokin' Joe Kubek with Dave Rubin

Texas blues guitar legend Smokin' Joe Kubek and acclaimed author and music historian Dave Rubin have teamed up to create this one-of-a-kind DVD/book bundle, featuring a high-definition DVD with Smokin' Joe himself demonstrating loads of electric blues licks, riffs, concepts, and techniques straight from his extensive arsenal. The companion book, co-written with Dave Rubin, provides standard notation and tablature for every smokin' example on the DVD, as well as bonus instructional material, and much more!
00696469 Book/DVD Pack $24.99

Blues You Can Use
by John Ganapes

A comprehensive source for learning blues guitar, designed to develop both your lead and rhythm playing. Covers all styles of blues, including Texas, Delta, R&B, early rock and roll, gospel, blues/rock and more. Includes 21 complete solos; extensive instruction; audio with leads and full band backing; and more!
00695007 Book/CD Pack $19.99

Blues You Can Use Chord Book
by John Ganapes

A reference guide to blues, R&B, jazz, and rock rhythm guitar, with hundreds of voicings, chord theory construction, chord progressions and exercises and much more. The Blues You Can Use Book Of Guitar Chords is useful for the beginner to advanced player.
00695082 .... $14.95

More Blues You Can Use
by John Ganapes

A complete guide to learning blues guitar, covering scales, rhythms, chords, patterns, rakes, techniques, and more. CD includes 13 full-demo solos.
00695165 Book/CD Pack $19.95

Blues Licks You Can Use
by John Ganapes

Contains music and performance notes for 75 hot lead phrases, covering styles including up-tempo and slow blues, jazz-blues, shuffle blues, swing blues and more! CD features full-band examples.
00695386 Book/CD Pack $16.95

HAL•LEONARD®
CORPORATION
7777 W. BLUEMOUND RD. P.O. BOX 13819 MILWAUKEE, WI 53213

www.halleonard.com
Prices, availability, and contents subject to change without notice.   Some products may not be available outside the U.S.A.

0313

TAB+

**Accurate Tabs
Gear Information
Selected Pedal Settings
Analysis & Playing Tips**

The Tab+ Series gives you note-for-note accurate transcriptions in notes and tab PLUS a whole lot more. These books also include performance notes to help you master the song, tips on the essential gear to make the song sound its best, recording techniques, historical information, right- and left-hand techniques and other playing tips – it's all here!

TAB. TONE. TECHNIQUE.

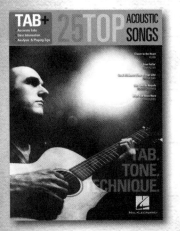

25 TOP ACOUSTIC SONGS

Big Yellow Taxi • Can't Find My Way Home • Cat's in the Cradle • The Clap • Closer to the Heart • Free Fallin' • Going to California • Good Riddance (Time of Your Life) • Hey There Delilah • A Horse with No Name • I Got a Name • Into the Mystic • Lola • Losing My Religion • Love the One You're With • Never Going Back Again • Norwegian Wood (This Bird Has Flown) • Ooh La La • Patience • She Talks to Angels • Shower the People • Tequila Sunrise • The Weight • Wild Horses • Wish You Were Here.
00109283 .... $19.99

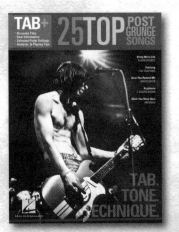

25 TOP CLASSIC ROCK SONGS

Addicted to Love • After Midnight • Another Brick in the Wall, Part 2 • Aqualung • Beat It • Brown Sugar • China Grove • Domino • Dream On • For What It's Worth • Fortunate Son • Go Your Own Way • Had to Cry Today • Keep Your Hands to Yourself • Life in the Fast Lane • Lights • Message in a Bottle • Peace of Mind • Reeling in the Years • Refugee • Rock and Roll Never Forgets • Roundabout • Tom Sawyer • Up on Cripple Creek • Wild Night.
00102519 .... $19.99

25 TOP HARD ROCK SONGS

Back in Black • Best of Both Worlds • Crazy Train • Detroit Rock City • Doctor, Doctor • Fire Woman • Hair of the Dog • In My Dreams • In-A-Gadda-Da-Vida • Jailbreak • Nobody's Fool • Paranoid • Rock Candy • Rock of Ages • School's Out • Shout at the Devil • Smoke on the Water • Still of the Night • Stone Cold • Welcome to the Jungle • Whole Lotta Love • Working Man • You've Got Another Thing Comin' • Youth Gone Wild • The Zoo.
00102469 .... $19.99

25 TOP METAL SONGS

Ace of Spades • Afterlife • Am I Evil? • Blackout • Breaking the Law • Chop Suey! • Cowboys from Hell • Down with the Sickness • Evil • Freak on a Leash • Hangar 18 • Iron Man • Laid to Rest • The Last in Line • Madhouse • Mr. Crowley • Psychosocial • Pull Me Under • Raining Blood • Roots Bloody Roots • Sober • Tears Don't Fall • Thunder Kiss '65 • The Trooper • Unsung.
00102501 .... $19.99

25 TOP POST-GRUNGE SONGS

All Star • Bawitdaba • Blurry • Boulevard of Broken Dreams • Bring Me to Life • Closing Time • Devour • Du Hast • Everlong • Far Behind • Hero • How You Remind Me • I Hate Everything About You • I Stand Alone • It's Been Awhile • Kryptonite • Metalingus • My Own Summer (Shove It) • One Last Breath • One Week • The Reason • Remedy • Sex and Candy • Thnks Fr Th Mmrs • Wish You Were Here.
00102518..$19.99

HAL•LEONARD®
CORPORATION
7777 W. BLUEMOUND RD. P.O. BOX 13819
MILWAUKEE, WISCONSIN 53213

www.halleonard.com

Prices, contents, and availability
subject to change without notice.

1013

GUITAR *signature licks*

Signature Licks book/CD packs provide a step-by-step breakdown of "right from the record" riffs, licks, and solos so you can jam along with your favorite bands. They contain performance notes and an overview of each artist's or group's style, with note-for-note transcriptions in notes and tab. The CDs feature full-band demos at both normal and slow speeds.

AC/DC
14041352 ....$22.99

ACOUSTIC CLASSICS
00695864 ....$19.95

AEROSMITH 1973-1979
00695106 ....$22.95

AEROSMITH 1979-1998
00695219 ....$22.95

DUANE ALLMAN
00696042 ....$22.99

BEST OF CHET ATKINS
00695752 ....$22.95

AVENGED SEVENFOLD
00696473 ....$22.99

BEST OF THE BEATLES FOR ACOUSTIC GUITAR
00695453 ....$22.95

THE BEATLES BASS
00695283 ....$22.95

THE BEATLES FAVORITES
00695096 ....$24.95

THE BEATLES HITS
00695049 ....$24.95

JEFF BECK
00696427 ....$22.99

BEST OF GEORGE BENSON
00695418 ....$22.95

BEST OF BLACK SABBATH
00695249 ....$22.95

BLUES BREAKERS WITH JOHN MAYALL & ERIC CLAPTON
00696374 ....$22.99

BLUES/ROCK GUITAR HEROES
00696381 ....$19.99

BON JOVI
00696380 ....$22.99

KENNY BURRELL
00695830 ....$22.99

BEST OF CHARLIE CHRISTIAN
00695584 ....$22.95

BEST OF ERIC CLAPTON
00695038 ....$24.95

ERIC CLAPTON – FROM THE ALBUM UNPLUGGED
00695250 ....$24.95

BEST OF CREAM
00695251 ....$22.95

CREEDANCE CLEARWATER REVIVAL
00695924 ....$22.95

DEEP PURPLE – GREATEST HITS
00695625 ....$22.95

THE BEST OF DEF LEPPARD
00696516 ....$22.95

THE DOORS
00695373 ....$22.95

TOMMY EMMANUEL
00696409 ....$22.99

ESSENTIAL JAZZ GUITAR
00695875 ....$19.99

FAMOUS ROCK GUITAR SOLOS
00695590 ....$19.95

FLEETWOOD MAC
00696416 ....$22.99

BEST OF FOO FIGHTERS
00695481 ....$24.95

ROBBEN FORD
00695903 ....$22.95

BEST OF GRANT GREEN
00695747 ....$22.95

BEST OF GUNS N' ROSES
00695183 ....$24.95

THE BEST OF BUDDY GUY
00695186 ....$22.99

JIM HALL
00695848 ....$22.99

JIMI HENDRIX
00696560 ....$24.95

JIMI HENDRIX – VOLUME 2
00695835 ....$24.95

JOHN LEE HOOKER
00695894 ....$19.99

HOT COUNTRY GUITAR
00695580 ....$19.95

BEST OF JAZZ GUITAR
00695586 ....$24.95

ERIC JOHNSON
00699317 ....$24.95

ROBERT JOHNSON
00695264 ....$22.95

BARNEY KESSEL
00696009 ....$22.99

THE ESSENTIAL ALBERT KING
00695713 ....$22.95

B.B. KING – BLUES LEGEND
00696039 ....$22.99

B.B. KING – THE DEFINITIVE COLLECTION
00695635 ....$22.95

B.B. KING – MASTER BLUESMAN
00699923 ....$24.99

THE KINKS
00695553 ....$22.95

BEST OF KISS
00699413 ....$22.95

MARK KNOPFLER
00695178 ....$22.95

LYNYRD SKYNYRD
00695872 ....$24.95

THE BEST OF YNGWIE MALMSTEEN
00695669 ....$22.95

BEST OF PAT MARTINO
00695632 ....$24.99

MEGADETH
00696421 ....$22.99

WES MONTGOMERY
00695387 ....$24.95

BEST OF NIRVANA
00695483 ....$24.95

THE OFFSPRING
00695852 ....$24.95

VERY BEST OF OZZY OSBOURNE
00695431 ....$22.95

BRAD PAISLEY
00696379 ....$22.99

BEST OF JOE PASS
00695730 ....$22.95

JACO PASTORIUS
00695544 ....$24.95

TOM PETTY
00696021 ....$22.99

PINK FLOYD – EARLY CLASSICS
00695566 ....$22.95

THE GUITARS OF ELVIS
00696507 ....$22.95

BEST OF QUEEN
00695097 ....$24.95

BEST OF RAGE AGAINST THE MACHINE
00695480 ....$24.95

RED HOT CHILI PEPPERS
00695173 ....$22.95

RED HOT CHILI PEPPERS – GREATEST HITS
00695828 ....$24.95

BEST OF DJANGO REINHARDT
00695660 ....$24.95

BEST OF ROCK 'N' ROLL GUITAR
00695559 ....$19.95

BEST OF ROCKABILLY GUITAR
00695785 ....$19.95

THE ROLLING STONES
00695079 ....$24.95

BEST OF JOE SATRIANI
00695216 ....$22.95

THE BEST OF SOUL GUITAR
00695703 ....$19.95

BEST OF SOUTHERN ROCK
00695560 ....$19.95

STEELY DAN
00696015 ....$22.99

MIKE STERN
00695800 ....$24.99

BEST OF SURF GUITAR
00695822 ....$19.95

BEST OF SYSTEM OF A DOWN
00695788 ....$22.95

ROBIN TROWER
00695950 ....$22.95

STEVE VAI
00673247 ....$22.95

STEVE VAI – ALIEN LOVE SECRETS: THE NAKED VAMPS
00695223 ....$22.95

STEVE VAI – FIRE GARDEN: THE NAKED VAMPS
00695166 ....$22.95

STEVE VAI – THE ULTRA ZONE: NAKED VAMPS
00695684 ....$22.95

STEVIE RAY VAUGHAN – 2ND ED.
00699316 ....$24.95

THE GUITAR STYLE OF STEVIE RAY VAUGHAN
00695155 ....$24.95

BEST OF THE VENTURES
00695772 ....$19.95

THE WHO – 2ND ED.
00695561 ....$22.95

JOHNNY WINTER
00695951 ....$22.99

NEIL YOUNG – GREATEST HITS
00695988 ....$22.99

BEST OF ZZ TOP
00695738 ....$24.95

HAL•LEONARD® CORPORATION
7777 W. BLUEMOUND RD. P.O. BOX 13819
MILWAUKEE, WISCONSIN 53213

www.halleonard.com

COMPLETE DESCRIPTIONS AND SONGLISTS ONLINE!
Prices, contents and availability subject to change without notice.